Date:

**973.7115 RUN
Runaway Slaves /**

Runaway Slaves

Other books in the History Firsthand series:

The Black Death
Castro's Cuba
The Civil War: The North
The Civil War: The South
The Constitutional Convention
Early Black Reformers
Explorers of the New World
The Gold Rush
The Great Depression
The Holocaust: Death Camps
Japanese American Internment Camps
Life Under Soviet Communism
Making and Using the Atomic Bomb
The Middle Ages
The Nuremberg Trial
The Oklahoma City Bombing
Pearl Harbor
Pioneers
Prohibition
The Renaissance
The Roaring Twenties
Sixties Counterculture
Slavery
The Vietnam War
War-Torn Bosnia
Women's Suffrage
The World Trade Center Attack

HISTORY
HF
FIRSTHAND

Runaway Slaves

Karin Coddon, *Book Editor*

Bonnie Szumski, *Publisher*
Scott Barbour, *Managing Editor*
David M. Haugen, *Series Editor*

GREENHAVEN
PRESS ®

TM

GALE

San Diego • Detroit • New York • San Francisco • Cleveland
New Haven, Conn. • Waterville, Maine • London • Munich

Cover credit: © Private Collection/Christie's Images/Bridgeman Art Library
Library of Congress, 19, 33, 150
North Wind Picture Archives, 110, 185

LIBRARY OF CONGRESS CATALOGING-IN-PUBLICATION DATA

Runaway Slaves / Karin Coddon, book editor.
   p. cm. — (History firsthand)
Includes bibliographical references and index.
ISBN 0-7377-1342-9 (lib. bdg. : alk. paper) —
ISBN 0-7377-1343-7 (pbk. : alk. paper)
   1. Underground railroad—Sources. 2. Fugitive slaves—United States—
Biography. 3. African American abolitionists—United States—Biography.
4. Quaker abolitionists—United States—Biography. 5. Antislavery movements—
United States—History—19th century—Sources. 6. Slavery—United States—
History—19th century—Sources. I. Coddon, Karin. II. Series.
E450.U516 2004
973.7'115—dc22
                                        2003061763

Contents

Foreword   9

Introduction: Fugitive Passage Along the
Underground Railroad   11

Chapter 1: Making the Break

Chapter Preface   27

1. The Perils of Recounting Escape Stories
by Frederick Douglass   29
The century's most eminent black abolitionist recounts his flight from slavery in 1838, with a word of
caution to those who would be too open in discussing
the details of escape.

2. How the Railroad Operated
by Charles A. Garlick   38
A former runaway describes conductors and stations
along his journey to freedom. He also speaks of the
slave hunters who sought escaped slaves for reward.

3. Toward a New Life in Canada
by James Adams   43
In recounting his escape north, a former slave dis-
cusses the intricate code of signals and subterfuges
employed by runaways and those who helped them.

4. Eluding the Slave Patrols
by Francis Henderson   53
A successful runaway, Henderson describes the near-
constant surveillance by patrols that sought to moni-
tor slaves' every movement off the plantations in order to prevent escape.

Chapter 2: Necessary Deceptions

Chapter Preface   59

1. An Unusual Escape
by Henry "Box" Brown   60
Slaves used a variety of methods to escape slavery.
One had himself nailed into a box and shipped to
freedom.

2. A Secret Hiding Place
by Harriet Jacobs 68

Fleeing her sexually abusive owner, Jacobs describes her initial escape to her grandmother's shed. There she ended up hiding for seven years before at last making her way north.

3. A Lie That Leads to Freedom
by Moses Roper 83

Roper, who would become a leading abolitionist, describes how posing as a full-blooded Native American facilitated his successful escape to the North.

4. A Daring Disguise
by William and Ellen Craft 94

Disguised as an elderly gentleman and his dutiful servant, a runaway couple are able to deflect suspicion as they travel openly from Georgia to freedom.

Chapter 3: Peril and Punishment

Chapter Preface 106

1. A Failed Escape
by William Wells Brown 107

The noted abolitionist recounts his first attempt to escape from slavery with his mother. The pair was recaptured, and tragically Brown's mother was sold to another master.

2. Boston Protests the Return of Anthony Burns to Slavery
by Charlotte Forten 114

The daughter of a prominent early black abolitionist recounts Boston's collective outrage over the apprehension, trial, and return to slavery of a Virginia runaway.

3. The Tragedy of Margaret Garner
by Levi Coffin 119

Captured by bounty hunters in the North, escaped slave Margaret Garner murders her infant daughter rather than see the child forced back into slavery.

4. Accused of Helping Runaway Slaves
by William Still 122

Samuel Green, a former slave who purchased his

freedom from his owner, is charged with abetting fugitive slaves (including his own son) as an agent of the Underground Railroad.

5. An Angry Crowd Rescues a Captive Fugitive Slave
by Sarah H. Bradford   128
In 1860, Harriet Tubman rallies protesters to rescue a fugitive slave from his captors.

Chapter 4: Conductors and Friends

Chapter Preface   134

1. A Friend of the Slaves
by Levi Coffin   135
The Quaker abolitionist details his and others' efforts to assist runaways in their escape to freedom. In his account, he assures hesitant Northerners that it is their moral duty to help fugitives.

2. The Underground Railroad in the Midwest
by Laura S. Haviland   146
Haviland details how she and fellow Quakers worked by "committee" to assist escaped slaves, often resorting to disguise and deception in order to thwart would-be captors.

3. Making the Case for Freedom
by Thomas Garrett   157
Abolitionist Garrett recounts a determined effort to help a black family legally establish its freedom through the courts.

5. The Trial of a Quaker Hero
by Harriet Beecher Stowe   160
The author of *Uncle Tom's Cabin* describes the ordeal of a young Quaker man imprisoned for helping slaves.

Chapter 5: Obstacles to Freedom

Chapter Preface   170

1. The Fugitive Slave Act
by the U.S. Congress   171
The text of the law enacted as part of the Compromise of 1850 mandates the return of runaway slaves

throughout the United States and its territories, weakens the legal recourse of fugitives, and prescribes punishment for those who aid and harbor them.

2. The Fugitive Slave Act Is Just
by Daniel Webster   180
The noted statesman and orator defends the rights of slaveholders to have their property returned, and he criticizes the abolitionists who abet runaways as well-meaning but fanatical lawbreakers.

3. A Fugitive Seems to Recant
by the Buffalo Commercial Advertiser, *the* Buffalo Morning Express, *and the* New York Daily Tribune   190
Several newspapers report a slave's apprehension by authorities and the obviously fabricated letter by which he apparently expresses his willingness to return to slavery in Kentucky, where slaves are in many cases "better off" than their free brethren in the North.

4. The Abduction of a Free Black Man
by Solomon Northup   200
A free black man living in Saratoga, New York, is kidnapped, drugged, and sold into slavery, demonstrating the grave dangers posed by the slave system to all blacks in the antebellum United States.

Chronology   209
For Further Research   215
Index   219

Foreword

In his preface to a book on the events leading to the Civil War, Stephen B. Oates, the historian and biographer of Abraham Lincoln, John Brown, and other noteworthy American historical figures, explained the difficulty of writing history in the traditional third-person voice of the biographer and historian. "The trouble, I realized, was the detached third-person voice," wrote Oates. "It seemed to wring all the life out of my characters and the antebellum era." Indeed, how can a historian, even one as prominent as Oates, compete with the eloquent voices of Daniel Webster, Abraham Lincoln, Harriet Beecher Stowe, Frederick Douglass, and Robert E. Lee?

Oates's comment notwithstanding, every student of history, professional and amateur alike, can name a score of excellent accounts written in the traditional third-person voice of the historian that bring to life an event or an era and the people who lived through it. In *Battle Cry of Freedom*, James M. McPherson vividly re-creates the American Civil War. Barbara Tuchman's *The Guns of August* captures in sharp detail the tensions in Europe that led to the outbreak of World War I. Taylor Branch's *Parting the Waters* provides a detailed and dramatic account of the American Civil Rights Movement. The study of history would be impossible without such guiding texts.

Nonetheless, Oates's comment makes a compelling point. Often the most convincing tellers of history are those who lived through the event, the eyewitnesses who recorded their firsthand experiences in autobiographies, speeches, memoirs, journals, and letters. The Greenhaven Press History Firsthand series presents history through the words of first-person narrators. Each text in this series captures a significant historical era or event—the American Civil War, the

Great Depression, the Holocaust, the Roaring Twenties, the 1960s, the Vietnam War. Readers will investigate these historical eras and events by examining primary-source documents, authored by chroniclers both famous and little known. The texts in the History Firsthand series comprise the celebrated and familiar words of the presidents, generals, and famous men and women of letters who recorded their impressions for posterity, as well as the statements of the ordinary people who struggled to understand the storm of events around them—the foot soldiers who fought the great battles and their loved ones back home, the men and women who waited on the breadlines, the college students who marched in protest.

The texts in this series are particularly suited to students beginning serious historical study. By examining these first-hand documents, novice historians can begin to form their own insights and conclusions about the historical era or event under investigation. To aid the student in that process, the texts in the History Firsthand series include introductions that provide an overview of the era or event, timelines, and bibliographies that point the serious student toward key historical works for further study.

The study of history commences with an examination of words—the testimony of witnesses who lived through an era or event and left for future generations the task of making sense of their accounts. The Greenhaven Press History Firsthand series invites the beginner historian to commence the process of historical investigation by focusing on the words of those individuals who made history by living through it and recording their experiences firsthand.

Introduction: Fugitive Passage Along the Underground Railroad

A mong the most striking examples of mass civil disobedience ever to occur in the United States, the Underground Railroad occupies a significant place in American history. Although African American slaves were denied the legal protections of citizenship and their owners' rights to recapture runaways were decreed by federal statute, countless citizens defied the law to assist fugitives to freedom, and even more slaves escaped abetted only by their own initiative and desire for liberty. While firm numbers are difficult to establish due to the Underground Railroad's necessary secrecy, it is believed that between the late eighteenth century and the outbreak of the Civil War in 1861, more than fifty thousand slaves successfully escaped bondage. Their destinations were almost as various as the railroad's routes that snaked unmarked throughout the slave states. Many fugitives fled to the Northern states, but thousands found havens in Canada, Mexico, the Caribbean, and across the Atlantic in Europe. They fled by foot, wagon, train, and ship, pursued by patrols, bounty hunters, and federal agents. Many were recaptured and faced harsh punishments that often included brutal beating, branding, or shackling, and resale to a distant owner entailing exile from family and community. Those who helped fugitives were also subject to legal penalties that ranged from stiff fines to terms of imprisonment. Yet knowing the risks, slaves continued to seek freedom and abolitionists both black and white continued to provide assistance.

In large part because of its covert and informal nature, the Underground Railroad has been both mythologized and misunderstood. On a literal level, the Underground Railroad was neither, but rather a loosely organized system of escape that utilized the terminology of rail travel—conductors, stations, and freight—to denote and encode the clandestine routes from slavery to freedom. Conductors were the individuals, often escaped slaves themselves like Harriet Tubman and William Wells Brown, who offered food, shelter, funds, and directions to runaways. Stations were the safe houses along the way to liberty where fugitives might be temporarily sheltered in attics, basements, and barns by abolitionists, out of sight from would-be captors who were frequently in close pursuit. The term *underground railroad* is believed to stem from an 1831 utterance made by a frustrated slave owner who, after losing sight of a fleeing bondman named Tice Davis at the Ohio River, is said to have complained that "it's as if he's gone off on some underground road."[1] Yet what is often overlooked in the vast and rich lore of the Underground Railroad is the extent to which fugitives sought and found safe passageway unassisted, traveling by night through swamps, fields, and back roads, or cleverly disguised. Thus the Underground Railroad is first and foremost a metaphor for any and all roads taken by slaves toward freedom. To acknowledge such is not to minimize the important role of the abolitionists who helped them, but rather to underscore the primacy of the will to be free that inspired so many bondmen and bondwomen to escape.

Early Underground Railroad scholars almost unanimously stressed the importance of Quaker conductors in assisting refugees from slavery along their journeys toward freedom. While there is no doubt that several prominent Quakers were vitally involved in harboring runaways (among them Levi Coffin, Thomas Garrett, and Lucretia Mott), historian Charles L. Blockson stresses that "Only a small minority of this religious community raised their voices against slavery and participated in the struggles to transport slaves to freedom."[2] Blockson points out that conductors were also to be found in other Christian communities, as well as among Jews and freethinkers. The scholarly weight given to the significance of white abolitionists owes as well to their authorship of many popular antebellum and post–Civil War Underground Railroad accounts, including Harriet Beecher Stowe's *Key to Uncle Tom's Cabin* (1853), Benjamin Drew's *A North-Side View of Slavery* (1856), Levi Coffin's *Reminiscences* (1876), and Wilbur H. Siebert's *Underground Railroad* (1898). Yet first-person escape narratives by Frederick Douglass, William Wells Brown, William and Ellen Craft, and Harriet Jacobs also found wide readerships. Black abolitionist William Still's *Underground Railroad Records*, published in 1872, predates Siebert's better-known work, and remains one of the most encyclopedic histories of the Railroad. In recent decades, historians have increasingly attended to the centrality—and heroism—of African Americans in the Underground Railroad as conductors, travelers, and chroniclers.

Origins of the Underground Railroad

Runaway slaves in North America date back to the introduction of African slavery into the colonies at Jamestown in 1619. Many early colonial slaves were also of Native American heritage, enslaved alongside white European indentured servants. But the African slave trade quickly supplanted other sources as the primary supplier of the cheap labor required by colonial planters to harvest their profitable crops of tobacco and sugar. In 1642 the Virginia colony passed a fugitive slave law penalizing those who abetted runaways. The criminalization of both escapes and their assistance indicates that such acts were already considered a problem in the mid-seventeenth-century American colonies. Many of the early colonial African slaves found refuge amid Native American tribes that welcomed them, sometimes with subsequent intermarriage and assimilation, other times, as with the Black Seminoles, with Africans maintaining a distinct cultural identity while living peaceably among the Indians. The Black Seminoles trace their lineage from African slaves who had fled south to Florida from the mid-Atlantic colonies. The Spanish, who still controlled much of Florida in the mid–seventeenth century, granted the Africans their liberty.

In the Northern colonies, some religious progressives, such as Quaker George Keith, raised objections to slavery. Keith published the colonies' first antislavery tract in 1693. Yet the Salem witch trials of 1692 were spurred by young girls' allegations that a slave woman from the Caribbean, Tituba, was practicing witchcraft, demonstrating that racial prejudice and fear coexisted in the early colonial North with the more enlightened views of men like George Keith.

However, the eighteenth century saw the gradual decline of slavery in the Northeast for economic as much as moral reasons. Sustained by bustling cities in New York, Pennsylvania, and Massachusetts, the Northern economy was coming to be as driven by manufacturing and trade as the Southern colonies were by agriculture and the slave labor that bolstered it. Recognizing the differing sectional interests even as they sought to "form a more perfect union," the constitutional framers largely sidestepped the issue of slavery lest an outright proscription preclude ratification by the Southern states. But several of the founders looked askance at the continued tolerance of legal slavery, none more so than Benjamin Franklin, a former slaveholder who served as president of the first American antislavery organization, the Pennsylvania Abolition Society, founded in 1775. Franklin continued to lobby for the abolition of slavery until his death in 1790, believing that the institution was a blight on a nation that claimed to be founded in virtue.

While Franklin's entreaties for the emancipation and education of enslaved African Americans went unheeded by the federal government, his home state, Pennsylvania, became the first to officially abolish slavery in 1780. Many historians also identify Philadelphia as the site of the first recorded Underground Railroad activity. In 1786 Quaker abolitionists helped several Virginia fugitives along their journey from bondage. A year later, a Quaker youth named Isaac T. Hopper devised a semiformal system by which to provide shelter and general assistance to fugitives. Hopper would go on to facilitate such aid organizations for runaway slaves in New York City as well as Pennsylvania.

The Emerging Black Community

Burgeoning black communities were also taking root in such
Northern cities as New York and Philadelphia. In the latter
city, minister Richard Allen, himself a fugitive slave, co-
founded (with Absalom Jones) the first black abolitionist
society in 1787 and the first Bethel African Methodist Episcopal Church in 1794, for which he ultimately served as
bishop. (Jones too founded a church, the African Protestant
Episcopal Church.) The black churches became the political
as well as religious centers of their communities, providing
not only houses of worship but also meeting places where
black Americans could discuss the pressing issues of the day.
Not surprisingly, the black church played a key role in abolitionist and Underground Railroad activities virtually from
its inception. As Charles Johnson and Patricia Smith observe,

> The black community played an essential role in harboring fugi-
> tives and educating them to the realities of their freedom. Vigi-
> lance committees circulated information about kidnappers and
> slave catchers and served as a source for food and medicine. When
> fugitive slaves were recaptured, the committees would organize
> rescue parties. This secretive network of abolitionists—both black
> and white—became known as the Underground Railroad.[3]

Yet while the initial stirrings of an official antislavery
movement were emerging in the new nation, proslavery interests were flexing their muscle with enactment of the first
federal Fugitive Slave Law in 1793, permitting owners or
their representatives to pursue and capture runaway slaves
even in free states and the territories. In the same year, Eli
Whitney's cotton gin was introduced into the agricultural
South, with the effect of vastly increasing production capacity and with it, the dependence of textile manufacturers
in both the North and Europe on Southern cotton. At the
dawn of the nineteenth century, slavery was becoming all
the more deeply entrenched in the Southern economy even
as it was disappearing from the North entirely.

The Fugitive Slave Law of 1793, while not as draconian as
the 1850 law, was an emphatic reminder to runaways that the

North offered only relative and precarious safety to them. By 1804 all the Northern states had abolished slavery, but fugitives were still subject to capture by owners or their agents. The War of 1812 against England also indirectly reinforced the appeal of Canada for many runaways, as veterans returning from campaigns in the English colony told of flourishing black communities north of the U.S. border, particularly in "Canada West," as the present-day province of Ontario was then known. Yet the Fugitive Slave Law notwithstanding, many black people, whether freeborn or runaways, chose to remain in the free states. Prejudice and discrimination plagued Northern blacks, but they drew strength and support from community life, holding down jobs, raising and supporting families, worshipping in church, and discussing politics in meeting halls. Thus while the proposal of colonization began to gain currency in 1816 among many Northern whites, including abolitionists, most blacks were vehemently opposed to the notion. Historian C. Peter Ripley describes the procolonization position and its rationale:

> The colonization movement was a mix of diverse interests that came together to settle free blacks and newly emancipated slaves in Africa. Most colonizationists believed that free blacks endangered American society. They accepted the popular myth that blacks lacked the moral character to become useful citizens. Even whites who considered slavery evil reasoned that sending blacks to a colony in Africa would ease white anxiety and thereby encourage manumissions, and at the same time provide free blacks with a refuge from American oppression. Most white abolitionists and antislavery organizations at the same time supported colonization. These gradual abolitionists theorized that emancipation would be achieved, gradually and peacefully, through the courts, individual manumissions, and the political system. Removing freed blacks would hasten the process, they believed.[4]

Steadfast in its conviction that the United States was as much homeland to black Americans as to whites, the black community mobilized against the colonization movement, staging mass protest meetings in New York, Boston, Philadelphia, and Baltimore. Black leaders such as David Walker and

William Watkins passionately decried the proposal to strip blacks of their national identity, and they urged resistance.

The colonization controversy raged throughout the 1820s and proved to be the catalyst for the emergence of an organized abolitionist movement. Black abolitionists managed to persuade their leading white counterpart, William Lloyd Garrison, who published the Boston antislavery newspaper the *Liberator*, to renounce colonization as counterproductive to the larger struggle for emancipation. In December 1833, sixty-two black and white abolitionists came together in Philadelphia to found the American Anti-Slavery Society. By persuading white abolitionists to recognize that colonization would only compound the injustices of bondage and oppression, black activists were pivotal in ushering in a radical new phase for the antislavery movement in which blacks and whites strove openly in an organized fashion to overthrow the institution of slavery. Nonetheless, tensions between black and white abolitionists persisted despite the mutual goal of emancipation and rejection of colonization. Some of these tensions were philosophical in basis: Garrison and his followers scorned the political arena in favor of passive resistance and "moral suasion" while many black abolitionists believed that emancipation could be achieved through the political system. Moreover, white abolitionists, although committed to the cause of black freedom, were often uncomfortable with the idea of *social* equality between the races, and treated their black colleagues condescendingly. Frederick Douglass, who was one of the greatest and most erudite orators in nineteenth-century public life, was incensed when white colleagues in the antislavery movement recommended that he keep "a little of the plantation speech"[5] in his addresses.

Most significantly, white antislavery activists regarded slavery as an abstract iniquity, but black abolitionists saw it as an all too tangible one, especially given the involvement of so many former slaves in the movement. As Charles Johnson and Patricia Smith observe, while white abolitionists focused their attention on a pervasive but somewhat distant evil, blacks were involved on a much more personal level. Although they were calling for the abolishment of an institution, they were also seeking justice for sons, brothers, mothers, fathers, sisters and grandmothers, uncles. There was very little room for negotiation when it came to the cause of freedom.[6]

Abolitionists and the Underground Railroad

Although in principle the official abolitionist organizations supported any and all actions undertaken in the name of the slave's liberty, they were not, for the most part, aligned with the more amorphous and secretive Underground Railroad. However, the various "vigilance committees" that had sprung up throughout the Northeast were deeply engaged in providing assistance to fugitive slaves. Black abolitionists such as David Ruggles, William Still, and Robert Purvis were especially active in vigilance committees, whose help included not only food and shelter but also aid in resettling in the free black community and, occasionally, even legal support against bounty hunters or pursuing owners. Many of the committee members were also conductors, including Still, his friend Joseph C. Bustill, and Syracuse minister J. W. Loguen, himself a fugitive slave.

The period between 1830 and 1865 comprises the peak years of Underground Railroad activities, due not only to the emergence of organized abolitionism but also to events in the South and the western territories. Major slave rebellions were relatively rare, but the 1831 insurrection led by Nat Turner in Southampton County, Virginia, in which around sixty whites were slain by Turner and his followers, resulted in even harsher treatment for slaves, stricter surveillance, and severe punishments for any perceived insubordination. As the risks of escape increased, so did its urgency for many bondmen and women. In the North, most abolitionists viewed Turner's actions as heroic (as they would John Brown's failed seizure of the armory at Harpers Ferry, Virginia, eighteen years later). The Turner insurrection sparked sometimes heated debate within the abolitionist movement about the question of violent resistance, but antislavery activists were in general agreement over the commitment to provide assistance to the oppressed in all nonviolent capacities. These included protests, petitions, and the circulation of pamphlets and other antislavery literature in the South. In response, proslavery Southerners complained vociferously over abolitionist "agitation" and the alleged interference in a legal institution. Slavery interests carried the day in the nation's capital, pressuring Congress in 1836 to enact a "gag rule" that served to postpone indefinitely all argument over antislavery petitions.

Undaunted, the abolitionists continued to make use of the public, if not political, sphere to get their antislavery message out to the populace. With increasing frequency fugitive slaves were adding their own voices, both in the lecture hall and the literary text, to the abolitionist cause. Frederick

Virginia slave Nat Turner is captured more than two months after leading a slave rebellion in which sixty whites were killed.

Douglass, William Wells Brown, Harriet Jacobs, and Solomon Northup were but a few of the onetime fugitives whose memoirs found wide and receptive audiences among the reading public. A dramatic high point of most slave narratives is the escape, where the protagonist manages to elude his or her would-be captors and after an arduous journey, at last reaches freedom. Benjamin Drew's *A North-Side View of Slavery* was a compilation of first-person accounts told by former slaves who had found new homes in Canada. It is fair to say that the Underground Railroad entered the popular American imagination by way of literature, although most slave narratives deliberately skimped on details of the flight from slavery lest disclosing precise information jeopardize future escape attempts. Harriet Beecher Stowe's phenomenally successful novel *Uncle Tom's Cabin*, which appeared in 1852, was embraced by a readership already acquainted with nonfictional accounts of slavery, and touched the hearts and minds of many white Northerners theretofore indifferent or undecided about the morality of the South's "peculiar institution."

The 1850 Fugitive Slave Act and Resistance

However, as influential as Stowe's novel and the slave narratives were in shaping public opinion and conveying the peril and daring of the Underground Railroad, it was the Fugitive Slave Act of 1850 that had the most dramatic and direct impact on the plight of runaways and those committed to helping them. The act augmented the Fugitive Slave Law of 1793 by mandating not only the right of owners, their agents, and federal authorities to seize runaways in free states but also the legal obligation of private citizens to assist in the recaptures. Those found guilty of helping fugitives faced strict fines and even imprisonment. The 1850 Fugitive Slave Act was cheered by Southern slave interests but roundly denounced throughout the North. Even Northerners who were unsympathetic to abolitionism resented the imposition of proslavery law onto their region. Free blacks as well as fugitives felt justifiably threatened by the act for its denial of most legal means by which an individual might establish his or her freedom in court, including the right to mount a defense and have a trial by jury. Where a generation before black abolitionists had decried colonization as an affront to their right to claim American identity, now many, such as pioneering journalist Mary Ann Shadd Cary, were exhorting blacks to emigrate, either openly or by way of the Underground Railroad, to Canada. As historians Richard Newman, Patrick Rael, and Philip Lapsansky observe,

> In addition to promising a relatively feasible site for relocation, Canada also offered a final refuge for African Americans who had fled slavery. As America's stringent fugitive slave laws increasingly rendered the lives of fugitives perilous, the sanctuary offered by Britain's avowedly antislavery legal codes grew ever more valued. Black settlements in Canada West, which began in earnest in the 1830s, provided opportunities for black leaders to demonstrate the capacity of African Americans for embodying ideals of independence and respectability.[7]

More than ever Underground Railroad activities were aimed toward shuttling runaways to Canada by way of stations in border regions of Vermont, New York, Michigan, and Wisconsin. While once again the exact number of Canadian emigrants is difficult to establish, it is believed that a minimum twenty-five thousand and perhaps as many as fifty thousand made the journey across the border.

Passionate resistance to the Fugitive Slave Act took place above ground as well as along the furtive northbound routes and way stations of the Underground Railroad. Ashtabula County, Ohio, was a particularly active Underground Railroad hub, and a December 1850 statement published in the county's newspaper made clear the citizens' intent to disregard the new federal slave statute: "The voice of the people is, Constitution or no Constitution, law or no law, no fugitive slave can be taken from the soil of Ashtabula County back to slavery. If anyone doubts this real sentiment, they can easily test it."[8] Throughout the North citizens not only

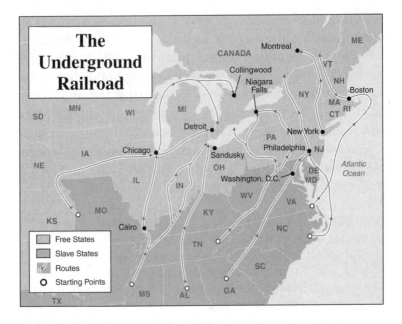

The Underground Railroad

Montreal
CANADA
Collingwood
Niagara Falls
Detroit
Chicago
Sandusky
Cairo
Washington, D.C.

Boston
New York
Philadelphia

ME
VT
NH
MA
RI
CT
NY
PA
NJ
DE
MD
VA
NC
SC
GA
AL
MS
TN
KY
WV
OH
IN
IL
MO
KS
NE
IA
WI
MN
SD
MI
TX

Atlantic Ocean

Free States
Slave States
Routes
O Starting Points

protested enforcement of "the odious Fugitive Slave Law," as Mary Ann Shadd Cary put it, but in several notable cases rallied to obstruct en masse attempts by federal officers or bounty hunters to seize fugitives. In 1851 a fugitive slave named Jerry Mchenry was openly rescued from bounty hunters who had tracked him to Syracuse by a group of abolitionists that included Gerritt Smith and William Seward, future secretary of state under Abraham Lincoln. The same year a riot broke out in Christiana, Pennsylvania, when a group of mostly black townspeople overcame agents of Maryland slave owner Edward Gorsuch to prevent the recapture of several fugitives. The aftermath of the Christiana riot left Gorsuch dead and another white man wounded. Thirty-six blacks and five whites were arrested and charged with treason for their flagrant violation of the Fugitive Slave Act. All were ultimately acquitted. Similar acts of collective civil disobedience occurred in Racine, Wisconsin, in 1854, with the rescue of Joshua Glover; in Ohio in 1858, where an angry crowd from the town of Oberlin stormed a hotel in nearby Wellington where John Price was being held by slave catchers from Kentucky; and in Troy, New York, in 1860, as

Harriet Tubman led a throng of citizens in freeing Charles Nalle from the clutches of U.S. marshals. Unlike fellow fugitives Mchenry, Glover, Price, and Nalle, Anthony Burns was forced back into slavery under the Fugitive Slave Act, but an estimated fifty thousand citizens took to the Boston streets in June 1854 to protest as armed federal officers ushered Burns to a southbound ship.

The Fugitive Slave Act, intended as a sop for Southerners disgruntled by abolitionist "agitation" and California's free status, served instead to fan the flames of outright defiance throughout the North. The act also intensified the "problem" that it purported to remedy, motivating more and more fugitives to flee to Canada and other foreign locales beyond the reach of American authorities and citizens, few though they were, now legally obliged to assist in the apprehension of runaway slaves. As historian James Oakes remarks, "By the 1850s runaways had become a major source of sectional antagonism solely because of the political conflict they both exposed and provoked. Far more directly than abolitionist propaganda, fugitive slaves forced both the North and South into ever-hardening defenses of their existing social structures."[9]

The Irreconcilable Conflict over Slavery

The failure of the Fugitive Slave Act to stem sectional tensions in the 1850s was compounded by two pivotal events toward the decade's end, events that seemed to underscore William Seward's term "irreconcilable conflict" in characterizing the North-South divide over slavery. In 1857 the Supreme Court, under the auspices of Chief Justice Roger Taney, ruled in the *Dred Scott* decision that the rights of citizenship did not apply to blacks, legalizing the reenslavement of former bondmen and women should they venture back into a slave state. *Dred Scott* essentially struck down all existing precedents that had sought to establish territorial balance between free and slave states, from the Missouri Compromise of 1821 to the Compromise of 1850, exceeding even the Kansas-Nebraska Act of 1854, which ruled that popular sovereignty should be the primary determinant of whether to allow slavery. The antislavery movement was both enraged and despairing. In 1859 militant abolitionist John Brown and a small band of followers seized temporary control over the federal arsenal at Harpers Ferry, Virginia, an audacious act that Brown hoped would incite a widespread slave insurrection. Brown's plan had taken shape with the support of several other antislavery activists, including William Lloyd Garrison, Harriet Tubman, and Gerritt Smith. After a bloody confrontation with federal forces Brown and his men were captured. Brown's subsequent execution elevated his status to a glorious martyr for the abolitionist cause. As for proslavery interests, the siege at Harpers Ferry confirmed their worst fears about the violent extremes to which abolitionist zealots would go in order to raze the institution of slavery.

The South reacted to Abraham Lincoln's election November 1860 as if John Brown had returned from the grave to finish the task aborted at Harpers Ferry. In fact, Lincoln was a relative moderate who vowed not to tamper with slavery where it already existed, much to the displeasure of abolitionists and Radical Republicans such as Senator Charles Sumner of Massachusetts and Congressman Thaddeus Stevens of Pennsylvania. In December 1860 South Carolina became first of ultimately eleven Southern states to secede from the United States in response to Lincoln's election. Five months later the newly formed Confederate States of America fired upon Fort Sumner, a Union installation in the harbor of Charleston, South Carolina, and the Civil War was under way.

The Underground Railroad continued its operations virtually until Robert E. Lee's surrender at Appomattox, Virginia, in April 1865. Many slaves sought refuge in Union army camps in Southern territory, even though the penalty for recapture was immediate execution. Harriet Tubman continued to venture into hostile territory to escort runaways out of bondage. She also served the Union troops as nurse, scout, and spy. Many fugitives who had fled the country in the immediate aftermath of the Fugitive Slave Act returned to the United States, often joining leading black activists such as Douglass and William Wells Brown in their calls for immediate emancipation, for the right for blacks to serve in the army, and for the vote. With the defeat of the Confederacy, slavery—and with it the Underground Railroad—came to a permanent end in the United States. But for black Americans, the struggle to claim the fruits of their hard-won freedom— full equality under the law, social integration, an end to racial discrimination and bigotry—remained ongoing. The mythic qualities of the Underground Railroad and its lore must not obscure its historical reality as an authentic if clandestine mass movement in which countless refugees from slavery risked and often gave their lives for freedom.

Notes

1. Quoted in Virginia Hamilton, *Many Thousand Gone: African Americans from Slavery to Freedom.* New York: Alfred A. Knopf, 2002, pp. 53–54.

2. Charles L. Blockson, *The Underground Railroad.* New York: Prentice-Hall, 1987, p. 230.

3. Charles Johnson, Patricia Smith, and the WGBH Series Research Team, *Africans in America: America's Journey Through Slavery.* New York: Harvest/Harcourt Brace, 1998, p. 367.

4. C. Peter Ripley, *Witness for Freedom.* Chapel Hill: University of North Carolina Press, 1993, p. 2.

5. Ripley, *Witness for Freedom,* p. 11.

6. Johnson et al., *Africans in America,* p. 370.

7. Richard Newman, Patrick Rael, and Philip Lapsansky, eds., *Pamphlets of Protest: An Anthology of Early African American Protest Literature, 1790–1860.* New York: Routledge, 2001, p. 198.

8. Quoted in Blockson, *The Underground Railroad,* p. 211.

9. James Oakes, "Fugitive Slaves Exacerbate the Sectional Crisis over Slavery," in *American Slavery.* Ed. William Dudley. San Diego: Greenhaven, 2000, pp. 223–24.

Chapter 1

Making
the Break

Chapter Preface

It is generally believed that the majority of runaway slaves were males between the ages of sixteen and thirty-five. Such a supposition, however, does not imply that the lot for female slaves was necessarily more tolerable, nor that bondwomen had any less keen a desire for freedom. Rather, male slaves were for the most part likelier to have opportunities for escape than their female counterparts. Bondmen were more frequently allowed to venture from their owners' property to run errands or even be leased to other masters or businesses that paid the slaves' wages to their owners. A slave charged with such responsibilities was already likely to have won a degree of trust from his owner that surely contributed to increased chances for escape. Indeed, the perception held by many whites of slaves' cheerful docility that helped spawn the "Sambo" stereotype was born of a calculated decision on the part of many bondmen and women. A guise of childlike simplicity and staunch loyalty to the master often served to deflect suspicion and thus to relax the stringent vigilance that otherwise dimmed the prospects for successful flight.

A slave deemed insubordinate or sullen, on the other hand, was subject to watchful supervision and seldom entrusted with privileges that might allow him or her occasional furloughs from the plantation. Owners feared not only escape but also organized slave insurrections, especially in the aftermath of the foiled Denmark Vesey conspiracy of 1822 and the Nat Turner uprising nine years later in Southampton County, Virginia. Vesey, a free black man, sought to provoke a mass rebellion by seizing arms from various arsenals in Charleston, South Carolina, to be distributed among the slaves who were his cohorts in the plot. The Turner rebellion left sixty whites and more than two hundred blacks dead before its leader, a slave apparently more motivated by religious fanaticism than antislavery zeal, was finally apprehended, and like Vesey, tried and executed. Many abolitionists both black and white were ambivalent about the effects of these uprisings, applauding the strike against the venal slave system while concerned that the subsequent harshening of slave codes and increased surveillance would impede the cause of freedom for both aspiring runaways and the antislavery movement as a whole.

The Perils of Recounting Escape Stories

Frederick Douglass

Frederick Douglass was the preeminent black abolitionist of the nineteenth century, famed as an orator, author, and editor of the antislavery newspaper the *North Star*. His influence extending beyond the abolitionist movement, Douglass was instrumental in pressuring President Abraham Lincoln to issue the Emancipation Proclamation in 1862 and to permit black soldiers to serve in the Union army during the Civil War. Although they frequently differed, especially over Lincoln's tendency to prefer cautious, incremental approaches to the slavery issue, Douglass was an invited guest to the president's second inauguration in 1864. Lincoln singled Douglass out for a special greeting and asked his opinion of the inaugural speech, observing "There is no man in the country whose opinion I value more than yours."

Douglass was himself a fugitive slave. Born Frederick Bailey, he served under a series of masters in his home state of Maryland. Sophia Auld, the wife of one of his last owners Hugh Auld, secretly taught the young Douglass to read and write, which was a crime in slave states. In September 1838, Douglass escaped to the Northeast. Soon thereafter he embarked upon his life as a free man (thought technically a fugitive) and abolitionist. In the following selection excerpted from his highly successful autobiography, Douglass describes

Frederick Douglass, *Narrative of the Life of Frederick Douglass: An American Slave, Written by Himself*. Boston: Anti-Slavery Office, 1845.

in general terms the circumstances of his escape, deliberately withholding key details lest they jeopardize other runaways. Douglass remained critical of former slaves who were less discreet in revealing their particular methods of escape, such as Henry "Box" Brown, whose arrangement to have himself shipped in a large crate to freedom quickly acquired a near-legendary status in the abolitionist community. He was also disturbed by the Underground Railroad for similarly advertising its successes. Equally telling is Douglass's admission of the pangs he endured upon leaving his loved ones behind. He suggests that the prospect of such a rupture from "the strong cords of affection" was as potent a deterrent to escape as the threats of punishment and bounty hunters.

I now come to that part of my life during which I planned, and finally succeeded in making, my escape from slavery. But before narrating any of the peculiar circumstances, I deem it proper to make known my intention not to state all the facts connected with the transaction. My reasons for pursuing this course may be understood from the following: First, were I to give a minute statement of all the facts, it is not only possible, but quite probable, that others would thereby be involved in the most embarrassing difficulties. Secondly, such a statement would most undoubtedly induce greater vigilance on the part of slaveholders than has existed heretofore among them; which would, of course be the means of guarding a door whereby some dear brother bondman might escape his galling chains. I deeply regret the necessity that impels me to suppress any thing of importance connected with my experience in slavery. It would afford me great pleasure indeed, as well as materially add to the interest of my narrative, were I at liberty to gratify a curiosity, which I know exists in the minds of many, by an accurate statement of all the facts pertaining to my most fortunate escape. But I must deprive myself of this pleasure, and the curious of the gratification which such a statement would afford. I would allow myself to suffer under the greatest

imputations which evil-minded men might suggest, rather
than exculpate myself, and thereby run the hazard of clos-
ing the slightest avenue by which a brother slave might clear
himself of the chains and fetters of slavery.

The Railroad's Flaw

I have never approved of the very public manner in which
some of our western friends have conducted what they call
the *underground railroad*, but which, I think, by their open
declarations, has been made most emphatically the *upper-
ground railroad*. I honor those good men and women for
their noble daring, and applaud them for willingly subject-
ing themselves to bloody persecution, by openly avowing
their participation in the escape of slaves. I, however, can
see very little good resulting from such a course, either to
themselves or the slaves escaping; while, upon the other
hand, I see and feel assured that those open declarations are
a positive evil to the slaves remaining, who are seeking to
escape. They do nothing towards enlightening the slave,
whilst they do much towards enlightening the master. They
stimulate him to greater watchfulness, and enhance his
power to capture his slave. We owe something to the slaves
south of the line as well as to those north of it; and in aiding the latter on their way to freedom, we should be careful
to do nothing which would be likely to hinder the former
from escaping from slavery. I would keep the merciless
slaveholder profoundly ignorant of the means of flight
adopted by the slave. I would leave him to imagine himself
surrounded by myriads of invisible tormentors, ever ready
to snatch from his infernal grasp his trembling prey. Let him
be left to feel his way in the dark; let darkness commensu-
rate with his crime hover over him; and let him feel that at
every step he takes, in pursuit of the flying bondman, he is
running the frightful risk of having his hot brains dashed out
by an invisible agency. Let us render the tyrant no aid; let us
not hold the light by which he can trace the footprints of our
flying brother. But enough of this. I will now proceed to the
statement of those facts, connected with my escape, for

which I am alone responsible, and for which no one can be made to suffer but myself.

Yearning for Freedom

In the early part of the year 1838, I became quite restless. I could see no reason why I should, at the end of each week, pour the reward of my toil into the purse of my master. When I carried to him my weekly wages, he would, after counting the money, look me in the face with a robber-like fierceness, and ask, "Is this all?" He was satisfied with nothing less than the last cent. He would, however, when I made him six dollars, sometimes give me six cents, to encourage me. It had the opposite effect. I regarded it as a sort of admission of my right to the whole. The fact that he gave me any part of my wages was proof, to my mind, that he believed me entitled to the whole of them. I always felt worse for having received any thing; for I feared that the giving me a few cents would ease his conscience, and make him feel himself to be a pretty honorable sort of robber. My discontent grew upon me. I was ever on the look-out for means of escape; and, finding no direct means, I determined to try to hire my time, with a view of getting money with which to make my escape. In the spring of 1838, when Master Thomas [Auld, brother-in-law of Hugh and owner of Douglass] came to Baltimore to purchase his spring goods, I got an opportunity, and applied to him to allow me to hire my time. He unhesitatingly refused my request, and told me this was another stratagem by which to escape. He told me I could go nowhere but that he could get me; and that, in the event of my running away, he should spare no pains in his efforts to catch me. He exhorted me to content myself, and be obedient. He told me, if I would be happy, I must lay out no plans for the future. He said, if I behaved myself properly, he would take care of me. Indeed, he advised me to complete thoughtlessness of the future, and taught me to depend solely upon him for happiness. He seemed to see fully the pressing necessity of setting aside my intellectual nature, in order to contentment in slavery. But in spite of him, and even in spite of myself, I continued to think, and to think about the injustice of my enslavement, and the means of escape.

About two months after this, I applied to Master Hugh for the privilege of hiring my time. He was not acquainted with the fact that I had applied to Master Thomas, and had been refused. He too, at first, seemed disposed to refuse; but, after some reflection, he granted me the privilege, and proposed the following term: I was to be allowed all my time, make all contracts with those for whom I worked, and find my own employment; and, in return for this liberty, I was to pay him three dollars at the end of each week; find myself in calking tools, and in board and clothing. My board was two dollars and a half per week. This, with the wear and tear of clothing and calking tools, made my regular expenses about six dollars per week. This amount I was compelled to make up, or relinquish the privilege of hiring my time.

Frederick Douglass

Rain or shine, work or no work, at the end of each week the money must be forthcoming, or I must give up my privilege. This arrangement, it will be perceived, was decidedly in my master's favor. It relieved him of all need of looking after me. His money was sure. He received all the benefits of slaveholding without its evils; while I endured all the evils of a slave, and suffered all the care and anxiety of a freeman. I found it a hard bargain. But, hard as it was, I thought it better than the old mode of getting along. It was a step towards freedom to be allowed to bear the responsibilities of a freeman, and I was determined to hold on upon it. I bent myself to the work of making money. I was ready to work at night as well as day, and by the most untiring perseverance and industry, I made enough to meet my expenses, and lay up a little money every week. I went on thus from May till August.

Master Hugh then refused to allow me to hire my time longer. The ground for his refusal was a failure on my part, one Saturday night, to pay him for my week's time. This failure was occasioned by my attending a camp meeting about ten miles from Baltimore. During the week, I had entered into an engagement with a number of young friends to start from Baltimore to the camp ground early Saturday evening; and being detained by my employer, I was unable to get down to Master Hugh's without disappointing the company. I knew that Master Hugh was in no special need of the money that night. I therefore decided to go to camp meeting, and upon my return pay him the three dollars. I stayed at the camp meeting one day longer than I intended when I left. But as soon as I returned, I called upon him to pay him what he considered his due. I found him very angry; he could scarce restrain his wrath. He said he had a great mind to give me a severe whipping. He wished to know how I dared go out of the city without asking his permission. I told him I hired my time, and while I paid him the price which he asked for it, I did not know that I was bound to ask him when and where I should go. This reply troubled him; and, after reflecting a few moments, he turned to me, and said I should hire my time no longer; that the next thing he should know of, I would be running away. Upon the same plea, he told me to bring my tools and clothing home forthwith. I did so; but instead of seeking work, as I had been accustomed to do previously to hiring my time, I spent the whole week without the performance of a single stroke of work. I did this in retaliation. Saturday night, he called upon me as usual for my week's wages. I told him I had no wages; I had done no work that week. Here we were upon the point of coming to blows. He raved, and swore his determination to get hold of me. I did not allow myself a single word; but was resolved, if he laid the weight of his hand upon me, it should be blow for blow. He did not strike me, but told me that he would find me in constant employment in future. I thought the matter over during the next day, Sunday, and finally resolved upon the third day of September, as the day upon which I would make a second attempt to secure my freedom. I now had three weeks during which to prepare for my journey. Early on Monday morning, before Master Hugh had time to make any engagement for me, I went out and got employment of Mr. Butler, at his ship-yard near the draw-bridge, upon what is called the City Block, thus making it unnecessary for him to seek employment for me. At the end of the week, I brought him between eight and nine dollars. He seemed very well pleased, and asked me why I did not do the same the week before. He little knew what my plans were. My object in working steadily was to remove any suspicion he might entertain of my intent to run away; and in this I succeeded admirably. I suppose he thought I was never better satisfied with my condition than at the very time during which I was planning my escape. The second week passed, and again I carried him my full wages; and so well pleased was he, that he gave me twenty-five cents, (quite a large sum for a slaveholder to give a slave,) and bade me to make a good use of it. I told him I would.

The Pain of Leaving Loved Ones

Things went on without very smoothly indeed, but within there was trouble. It is impossible for me to describe my feelings as the time of my contemplated start drew near. I had a number of warm-hearted friends in Baltimore,—friends that I loved almost as I did my life,—and the thought of being separated from them forever was painful beyond expression. It is my opinion that thousands would escape from slavery, who now remain, but for the strong cords of affection that bind them to their friends. The thought of leaving my friends was decidedly the most painful thought with which I had to contend. The love of them was my tender point, and shook my decision more than all things else. Besides the pain of separation, the dread and apprehension of a failure exceeded what I had experienced at my first attempt. The appalling defeat I then sustained returned to torment me. I felt assured that, if I failed in this attempt, my case would be a hopeless one—it would seal my fate as a slave forever. I could not hope to get off with any thing less than the severest punishment, and being placed beyond the means of escape. It required no very vivid imagination to depict the most frightful scenes through which I should have to pass, in case I failed. The wretchedness of slavery, and the blessedness of freedom, were perpetually before me. It was life and death with me. But I remained firm, and, according to my resolution, on the third day of September, 1838, I left my chains, and succeeded in reaching New York without the slightest interruption of any kind. How I did so,—what means I adopted,—what direction I travelled, and by what mode of conveyance,—I must leave unexplained, for the reasons before mentioned.

Freedom and Loneliness

I have been frequently asked how I felt when I found myself in a free State. I have never been able to answer the question with any satisfaction to myself. It was a moment of the highest excitement I ever experienced. I suppose I felt as one may imagine the unarmed mariner to feel when he is rescued by a friendly man-of-war from the pursuit of a pirate. In writing to a dear friend, immediately after my arrival at New York, I said I felt like one who had escaped a den of hungry lions. This state of mind, however, very soon subsided; and I was again seized with a feeling of great insecurity and loneliness. I was yet liable to be taken back, and subjected to all the tortures of slavery. This in itself was enough to damp the ardor of my enthusiasm. But the loneliness overcame me. There I was in the midst of thousands, and yet a perfect stranger; without home and without friends, in the midst of thousands of my own brethren—children of a common Father, and yet I dared not to unfold to any one of them my sad condition. I was afraid to speak to any one for fear of speaking to the wrong one, and thereby falling into the hands of money-loving kidnappers, whose business it was to lie in wait for the panting fugitive, as the ferocious beasts of the forest lie in wait for their prey. The motto which I adopted when I started from slavery was this—"Trust no man!" I saw in every white man an enemy, and in almost every colored man cause for distrust. It was a most painful situation; and, to understand it, one must needs experience it, or imagine himself in similar circumstances. Let him be a fugitive slave in a strange land—a land given up to be the hunting-ground for slaveholders—whose inhabitants are legalized kidnappers—where he is every moment subjected to the terrible liability of being seized upon by his fellowmen, as the hideous crocodile seizes upon his prey!—I say, let him place himself in my situation—without home or friends—without money or credit—wanting shelter, and no one to give it—wanting bread, and no money to buy it,—and at the same time let him feel that he is pursued by merciless men-hunters, and in total darkness as to what to do, where to go, or where to stay,—perfectly helpless both as to the means of defence and means of escape,—in the midst of plenty, yet suffering the terrible gnawings of hunger,—in the midst of houses, yet having no home,—among fellow-men, yet feeling as if in the midst of wild beasts, whose greediness to swallow up the trembling and half-famished fugitive is only equalled by that with which the monsters of the deep swallow up the helpless fish upon which they subsist,—I say, let him be placed in this most trying situation,—the situation in which I was placed,—then, and not till then, will he fully appreciate the hardships of, and know how to sympathize with, the toil-worn and whip-scarred fugitive slave.

How the Railroad Operated

Charles A. Garlick

Because of the importance of secrecy to the Underground
Railroad, many of the more detailed descriptions of its operations appeared retrospectively, especially in the decades
immediately following the Civil War. One such account was
composed by Charles A. Garlick, who published his autobiography in 1902. The following selection from Garlick's
memoir conveys how closely those involved in the Underground Railroad, black and white alike, worked in concert to
help runaways navigate the journey from the South to the
North or to Canada. Specifically, Garlick and the white abolitionist whose name the former Abel Bogguess adopted in
tribute, continued to assist fugitives even after the author's
own successful escape. Garlick's account also demonstrates
the constant threat posed by bounty hunters through their regular incursions into free states in pursuit of their quarry.

I, ABEL BOGGUESS, now CHARLES A. GARLICK,
was born near Shinnston, West Virginia, about the middle of February, 1827, on the plantation of Richard Bogguess.
My parents were slave laborers on the farm, my mother having charge of the household. Mr. Bogguess was a bachelor
owning some three hundred acres of land in Harrison
County, and his brother owned five hundred acres adjoining. I had eleven brothers and sisters, nine of whom were
living in 1843, when I left the old home for the North and

Charles A. Garlick, *Life, Including His Escape and Struggle for Liberty, of Charles A.
Garlick, Born a Slave in Old Virginia, Who Secured His Freedom by Running Away from
His Master's Farm in 1843.* Jefferson, OH: J.A. Howells & Company, 1902.

that freedom I so often dreamed of.

As will be seen I was then sixteen years old and it was fully forty years after I threw off the yoke of bondage and became a freeman, before I again saw any members of my immediate family, except an elder brother, Rawley Bogguess Johnson, who took his departure from our Virginia home a day or two before I did, and subsequently found a home in Uniontown, Fayette Co., Pennsylvania. Rawley married prior to his leaving Virginia, and took his wife and children with him, and later located in Youngstown where his children still live.

Richard Bogguess died some four months prior to my leaving home, leaving a will which, it was understood, made his colored people free. The administrator, one George Harter, left the same day I did to visit Fairmount, the county seat, ten miles away, to probate the will. I had little confidence that I would secure the freedom I sought through the provisions of the will, and found subsequently that I was right, for the will was contested.

The Family Sets Off for Freedom

It was Saturday when mother, five of the smaller children and myself left the old plantation which had been our home, and traveled northward a distance of fifteen miles, reaching William Heffin, an old neighbor's hospitable home not far from midnight. He took us in and after we had eaten he gave us a loaf of bread. We then left at once for more secure quarters in a dense wood where we found refuge on the summit of a huge rock, which we reached by climbing a moss-covered log or tree trunk leaning against it. There we remained until the following Monday morning, I keeping watch and seeing those who were in pursuit of us return footsore and weary to the plantation. Uncle Elijah Bogguess and Tom McIntyre found our retreat, Sunday night, and coming to us, advised mother to return with the children as the will would probably stand I was advised to continue my search for freedom, and before dawn I bade my mother and the children goodbye, and started on the long and dangerous trip for that haven where slavery was unknown.

Help from the Underground Railroad

The underground railroad was brought into use wherever practicable, there being occasional stations where I was assisted to elude my pursuers and sent ahead when safety was assured. Just one week's time was consumed in reaching Uniontown, where agents of the underground railroad at the ferry in Greensburg instructed me to go. There I lay concealed in the haymow of a zealous friend of my race, who provided me with food until an opportunity offered three days later for me to continue my journey. Just after dark, I mounted a fleet horse, which my host had provided, and under a strong escort I reached the National road. Accompanied by a faithful mounted guard I rode rapidly towards Pittsburgh, which I reached the following night. Leaving my friend to return with the horses, I hastened forward on foot some seven miles to the smoky city.

J.B. Vashong and Thomas McKeever, father of the late Mrs. Thos. Guy, then kept a regular station on the underground and here I found refuge for three days. He as a gentleman of wealth, and hundreds of my race have cause to bless his memory for the generous aid accorded them in their efforts to find freedom Samuel Marshall, [of] Butler Co., some fifteen miles away, kept another station and I next journeyed there under his guidance and remained for a week at his house resting. Then I was sent to a relative of his, John Rainbow, at New Castle, where I found refuge at Rev. Bushnell's, who had a brother in Cherry Valley. Next I tramped to Amos Chews in Brookfield, and the following morning left for Hartford, Trumbull Co., where I found kind friends in the persons of Ralph Plumb and Seth Hayes, merchants, in whose cheese warehouse I worked for two weeks. Learning that some southerners, presumably in search of runaway slaves, were in the vicinity, I left hastily, bringing up at Stod Stevens' store in Gustavus, remained there over night and the following morning left in company with Joseph B. Barber, cattle dealer of Wayne, who turned me over to George Quick, who brought me in a buggy to Alba Coleman, agent underground railroad, at West Andover. Arrived there Saturday night and remained until Monday afternoon. I then left on foot, reaching Anson Kirby Garlick's hospitable home an hour later.

After a night with him, I was proposing to continue my journey to Canada when he advised me to remain with him and go to school. In the South I had not attended school two days when the master found it out and forbade my further efforts to secure an education.

An Opportunity for Education

I remained with Mr. Garlick from 1843 to 1846 attending district school a portion of the time during the winter, working on the place the rest of the time.

The first winter I attended school. I was awarded the second prize for the greatest improvement in writing. Miss Sophia Houghton, an elder sister of the late Mrs. Judge Betts, of Jefferson, taking the first prize.

On accepting Mr. Garlick's hospitality and home, he addressed me as "Charley" and becoming known as Charley Garlick, I, at my benefactor's suggestion, adopted this the name I have ever since borne. About my first work at my new home was grading the lawn, and here I learned the northern method of driving oxen by the "Haw and Gee" method. In the South cattle are guided with a rope hitched to one horn, and I presume no one ever made a more awkward spectacle than I did during my first efforts with that lively team of young steers. I, however, conquered, and a creditable job was the result. I did so well that I was next put to clearing up several acres of land on the farm now owned by Dwight Carpenter.

Encounters with Runaways and Slave Hunters

In '46 Mr. Garlick and myself went East in search of my brother, whom we thought was in Butler County. At Gurdy's Run near Pittsburgh we encountered a camp meeting, and here we soon found ourselves in hot water. The impression obtained that Mr. Garlick was a slave holder and was using me as a decoy to obtain possession of my brothers, who were living in the vicinity of Mr. Marshall's. We were both made prisoners, but on Mr. Garlick's producing a paper upon which was the name of Deacon Hubbard, of Ashtabula, a lake terminus of the underground railroad, he was allowed to depart, they escorting him from the camp ground to assure his going. I escaped the same night and made my way to Squire Marshall's where I was delighted to find my brothers. I remained there one year before returning to Ohio.

At the close of my year's labor an episode occurred which created great excitement in the vicinity. There was at that time a dozen or more colored men about there who had taken "French leave" of their old masters and were at work for the farmers. One day as I was hitching up the horses after dinner to resume my work, I suddenly discovered a group of horsemen, thirteen in number, whom I recognized as slaveholders by the broad-brim hats they wore.

I at once apprised Mr. Marshall and, turning over the team to him, started on a run to notify the colored boys of their danger. The cavalcade spurred after me with cries of "stop him," "stop him," but I turned into a ravine and eluded them, and gave the alarm which soon brought together a squad of eight persons, two of whom were white. Some had shotguns and others clubs, while the slaveholders were armed with Colts revolvers. When they came up a parley occurred during which some hot talk ensued, our party ordering the others to leave or take the contents of the guns, as such as they were not wanted in Pennsylvania, nor anywhere else for that matter. They finally left, and as they rode away, one of our party fired his gun into the air which greatly hastened the speed of the retiring party, who were not heard of again.

Squire Marshall inserted a notice in the papers warning them that, if they came again, they would meet with a warm reception and hospitable graves. This ended the last raid of the slave holding, slave-catching cohorts to that station of the underground railroad.

Toward a New Life in Canada

James Adams

Benjamin Drew was a Boston abolitionist whose book *Testimony of the Canadian Fugitives* (1850) became one of the richest sources of runaway slave accounts in antebellum America. Sponsored by the Canadian Anti-Slavery Society and abolitionist John P. Jewett, Drew's book was based on interviews he had conducted throughout Canada with more than a hundred former slaves who had successfully ridden the Underground Railroad to freedom. Canada had abolished slavery in 1833, and its shared border and accessible ports in Windsor and New Brunswick made it a natural destination for runaways, especially after the 1850 Fugitive Slave Law rendered even liberal New England a less than secure haven. It has been estimated that around forty thousand fugitives had made their way to Canada by the time of the Civil War.

The following selection, attributed by Drew to James Adams, describes the arduous northward journey undertaken by young Adams, his cousin, Ben, and a group of other runaways fleeing slavery in Virginia. Adams's expression of hope for a new life as a free man speaks for the yearnings of all fugitives seeking the "promised land" north of the United States in Canada.

I was raised in Virginia, about twenty miles above the mouth of the Big Kanawha. At the age of seventeen, I set out to seek freedom in company with Benjamin Harris,

Benjamin Drew, *A North-Side View of Slavery. The Refugee; or The Narratives of Fugitive Slaves in Canada Related by Themselves*. Boston: John P. Jewett and Company, 1856.

(who was a cousin of mine,) and a woman and four children. I was young, and they had not treated me very badly; but I had seen older men treated worse than a horse or a hog ought to be treated; so, seeing what I was coming to, I wished to get away. My father being overseer, I was not used so badly as some even younger than myself, who were kicked, cuffed, and whipped very badly for little or nothing. We started away at night, on the 12th of August, 1824. After we had crossed the river, alarm was given, and my father came down where we had crossed, and called to me to come back. I had not told my intention to either my father or mother. I made no answer at all, but we walked three miles back from the river, where we lay concealed in the woods four days.

A Helping Hand

The nights we passed at the house of a white friend; a friend indeed. We set out on a Monday night, and on the night following, seven more of my fellow-servants started on the same race. They were overtaken on Wednesday night, while they were in a house on the Ohio side. One jumped from a window and broke his arm; he stayed in the woods some days, and then he returned. The other six, two women and four children, were carried back, and the man we stopped with told us that the two women were whipped to make them tell where we were, so they could come upon us. They told their master as near as they could. On Thursday five white men came to the house where we had been concealed, but we were then in the woods and mountains, three miles from the friend's house. Every evening, between three and four o'clock, he would come and bring us food. We had nothing to give him—it was the hand of Divine Providence made him do it. He and others on the river see so much abuse of colored people that they pity them, and so are ready to give them aid; at least it was so then. He told the white men he knew nothing about us, and nothing of the kind. They searched his premises, and then left, believing his story. He came to us and said, "Boys, we are betrayed, they are coming now round the hill after us." We picked up our bundles and started on a run; then he called us back, and said he did it to try our *spunk*. He then told us of those who were carried back, and of the searching of his premises. We lodged in his barn that night. On the morning of Friday, he took us twelve miles to a place where the woman would have to leave her children, because he could conceal her better without them. He pointed out a house occupied by a family of Methodists, where she could go and tell them she was going back, and so leave her children there. But when she reached the house the father and mother were absent, so she went at a venture to another house. As it was raining and dark, she was guided by a white boy, a stout lad, and a girl with a lantern. At this house, she slept on a pallet on the floor; and when all else were asleep, she put her baby, which she had all along kept in her arms, into her oldest boy's care, crept to the door and went out. We had bidden her good-by, not expecting to see her.

A Betrayal

When the boy and girl had come back from guiding her, I heard the boy say, "Now we shall get fifty dollars for giving her up, and she'll get a good fleecing into the bargain." The man where we had stopped intended to take her to his house after she had got rid of her children, and when opportunity offered, send her to Canada. We went to a fire which we saw burning in a clearing, and Ben slept while I kept watch. Presently the woman came towards us. I heard the cracking of sticks as she came, and awoke Ben. He raised a sort of tomahawk he had made, intending to strike the person approaching, supposing it was an enemy. Said she, "Oh Ben, don't strike me, it is I." This made me cry to think Ben was so near killing the woman. Then she begged us not to leave her until the man should come to find her. He not coming so soon as we expected, we all steered back the twelve miles through the woods. Towards night, we heard his cow-bells; we drove the cattle before us, knowing that they would go home. Just as they had guided us there, the man, who had also followed the bells, came up. He told us that the children had been carried back to their master. We supposed the boy—guide—had betrayed them, but do not know. We stayed in his barn all night, and left on Sunday morning, the woman remaining behind.

At about noon, we were near a village. He pointed out a haystack, where we were to rendezvous at night, to meet another man whom our friend was to send to take us further along on our way. At night we went to the haystack; a road ran by it. Instead of keeping watch by the stack, we were so jaded that we crossed the road and lay down to rest on the bare ground, where we fell asleep. The man, as we afterwards learned from him, came as agreed upon, whistled and made signals, but failed to wake us up. Thinking we had been pursued away, he went back without us. The next morning, when we awoke, the sun was rising red, right on the public road. We saw a man at his door some two hundred yards from us. I went to ask him how the roads ran; Harris told me to inquire the way to Carr's Run, near home, so we would go the contrary. By the time I got back, Ben, who had watched, saw the man leave his house with his gun, and take a circle round to come down on us; but before he could head us, we were past him in the road running. We ran and walked about four miles barefoot; then we took courage to put on our shoes, which we had not dared stop long enough to do before, for fear the man with the gun would get ahead of us.

More Conductors and Pursuers

We were now on the top of a high hill. On our right was a path leading into the woods. In this path we descended, and after walking a few minutes, we arrived at a house by the main road. We went in to ask for a drink of buttermilk. Only the woman of the house was at home. Said she, "Boys, you are the very ones my husband was looking for last night." We denied it, being right on the road, and afraid. She insisted, "for," said she, "the man who came to tell my husband, said there was a big one and a little one." I was the little one. She gave us crackers, cheese, and onions. Against her advice, we left the house and moved on. Presently we came to a toll-gate, about which there were standing several white men. We walked up boldly to the gate; one of the men then asked us, "Where are you going?" Ben answered, "We are going to Chillicothe to see our friends there." Then he made answer and said, "You can't go any further, you must go back with me, you are the very boys I was looking for last night." We told him we wanted to go on, but he said, "There are so many buckskin Yankees in these parts that you will be taken before you get half through the town." We then went back to his house, but we did not stop more than ten minutes, because it would be dangerous for him as well as for us if we were caught on his premises. He stuck up a pole close to his house and tied a white cloth on it; then he led us up to the top of the hill (this was Monday, quite early in the morning), and showed us a rough place of bushes and rocks where we could lie concealed quite pleasantly, and so high up that we could see the main road, and the toll-gate, and the house, and the white flag. Said he, "If there's any danger, I'll send a child out to throw down the white flag; and if you get scared away from here, come back at night and I'll protect you." Soon after he left us, we saw five white men come to his house on horseback; they were the five who had carried back the others that tried to escape. Two of them went into the house; then we saw a little girl come out and climb up on the fence, as if she were playing about, and she knocked down the flag-pole—which meant that we were to look out for ourselves. But we did not feel that there was any immediate danger, and so we kept close under cover. Pretty soon the two came out of the house, and they all rode forward very fast, passed the toll-gate, and were soon out of sight. I suppose they thought to overtake us every minute, but luckily I have never seen them since. In the evening the man came and conducted us to his house, where we found the men we had seen at the toll-gate in the morning. They were mostly armed with pistols and guns. They guided us to a solitary house three miles back among the mountains, in the neighborhood of which we remained three days. We were told to go up on the mountain very high, where was an Indian cave in the rocks. From this cave we could look a great distance around and see people, and we felt afraid they would see us. So instead of staying there, we went down the mountain to a creek where trees had been cut down and branches thrown over the bank; we went under the branches and bushes where the sand was dry, and there we would sit all day. We all the time talked to each other about how we would get away, and what we should do if the white folks tackled us; that was all our discourse.

Through the Wilderness

We stayed there until Friday, when our friends gave us knapsacks full of cakes and dried venison, and a little bundle of provision besides, and flints and steel, and spunk, and a pocket-compass to travel through the woods by. We knew the north-star, but did not travel nights for nearly a week. So on Friday morning we set out, the men all bidding us goodby, and the man of the flag-staff went with us half a day to teach us the use of the compass; we had never seen one before. Once in a while he would put it on a log to show us how to travel by it. When he was leaving us, he took his knife and marked on the compass, so that we should steer a little west of north.

During the six days succeeding, we traversed an unbroken wilderness of hills and mountains, seeing neither man nor habitation. At night we made a fire to sit by. We saw deer on our way; we were not annoyed by wild animals, and saw but one snake, a garter-snake. The first sign of man we met with was a newly-made road; this was on the seventh day from the time we left the house in the mountains. Our provisions held out well, and we had found water enough. After crossing the road, we came out from the mountains to a level cleared place of farms and houses. Then we were afraid, and put ourselves on our guard, resolving to travel by night. We laid by until starlight, then we made for a road leading to the north. We would follow a road until it bent away from the north; then we would leave it and go by the compass. This caused us to meet many rivers and streams where there were no bridges; some we could wade over, and some we crossed by swimming. After reaching the clearings, we scarcely dared build a fire. Once or twice we took some green corn from the fields, and made a brush fire to roast it. After lighting the fire, we would retire from it, as far almost as we could see it, and then watch whether anybody might come to it. When the fire had gone out, the corn would be about done.

Our feet were now sore with long travelling. One night we came to a river; it was rather foggy, but I could see a ferry-scow on the other side. I was afraid of alligators, but I swam over and poled the scow back and ferried Ben across—his ankle was so sore, that he did not like to put his foot in the water if he could help it. We soon reached an old stable in the edge of a little town; we entered it and slept alternately one keeping watch, as we always managed while in the neighborhood of settlements. We did not do this in the wilderness—*there* we slept safely and were quite *reconciled.* At cock-crowing in the morning we set out and went into the woods, which were very near; there we stayed through the day.

Another Friend and Guide

At night we started on and presently came into a road running north-west. Coming to a vine patch we filled our knapsacks with cucumbers; we then met a white man, who asked us, "Which way are you travelling?" My cousin told him "To Cleveland, to help a man drive a drove of cattle." He then said, "I know you must be runaways, but you needn't be afraid of me—I don't want to hurt you." He then told us something that we knew before—that the last spring five fugitives were overtaken at his house by my master and two other men; that the fugitives took through his wheat-field— one of them, a little fellow, could not run so fast as the rest, and master called to him to stop, or he'd shoot him. His answer was, "shoot and be d—d!" The man further told us, that he took through the wheat-field as if he would assist in catching the slaves, but that when he got near enough, he told them to "push on!" Ben and I knew about the pursuit, and what the little fellow had said; for it got round among the servants, after master got back. That little fellow's widow is now my wife. We went to the man's house, and partook of a good luncheon. He told us to hurry, and try to get through Newark before daylight. We hurried accordingly, but it was daybreak when we crossed the bridge. We found the little toll-gate open and we went through—there were lights in a tavern window at the left of the gate, and the windows had no curtains. Just as we were stepping off the bridge, a plank rattled, then up started after us a little black dog, making a great noise. We walked smartly along, but did not run until we came to a street leading to the right, then we ran fast until we came to a left hand turn, which led to the main road at the other side of the town. Before sunrise, we hid in a thicket of briars, close by the road, where we lay all day, seeing the teams, and every thing that passed by.

Securing Passage to Canada

At dark we went on again, passed through Mount Vernon in the night, and kept on until daylight. Again we halted in concealment until night, then we went on again through Wooster. After leaving Wooster, we saw no more settlements, except one little village, which we passed through in broad day. We entered a store here, but were asked no questions. Here we learned the way to Cleveland. In the middle of the afternoon we stopped for a little rest. Just before night we moved forward again and travelled all night. We then stopped to rest until four in the afternoon, meanwhile roasting some corn as before. At about four, we met a preacher, who was just come from Cleveland. He asked us if we were making our escape—we told him "No." He said, "You need not be afraid of me, I am the friend of all who travel from the South to the North." He told us not to go into Cleveland, as we would be taken up. He then described a house which was on our way, where, he said, we might mention our meeting him, and we would find friends who would put us on board a boat. We hid until dark, then we went to the house, which we recognized readily from the preacher's description. We knocked at the door, and were invited in. My cousin told them what the minister had said. The man of the house hid us in his barn two nights and three days. He was a shoemaker. The next night after we got there, he went to Cleveland himself to get a berth for us aboard some boat for Canada. When he returned, he said he had found a passage for us with Capt. B., who was to sail the next Thursday at 10 P.M. At that hour we embarked, having a free passage in a schooner for Buffalo. On board this boat, we met with an Englishman whom we had often seen on a steamboat at the plantation. He knew us, and told us a reward of one hundred dollars was offered for each of us, and he showed us several handbills to that effect. He said they had been given him to put up along the road, but he had preferred to keep them in his pocket. Capt. B. took away our knives and Ben's tomahawk, for fear of mischief.

We reached Buffalo at 4 P.M. The captain said, that if there was any danger in the town, he would take us in his yawl and put us across. He walked through the town to see if there were any bills up. Finding no danger, he took us out of the hatchway—he walked with us as far as Black Rock Ferry, giving us good advice all the way, how we should conduct ourselves through life in Canada, and we have never departed from his directions—his counsel was good, and I have kept it.

A New Home and Freedom

I am now buying this place. My family are with me—we live well, and enjoy ourselves. I worship in the Methodist church. What religious instruction I received on plantation, was from my mother.

I look upon slavery as the most disgusting system a man can live under. I would not be a slave again, except that I could not put an end to my own existence, through fear of the punishment of the future.

Men who have never seen or felt slavery cannot realize it

for the thing it is. If those who say that fugitives had better go back, were to go to the South and *see* slavery, they would never wish any slave to go back.

I have seen separations by sales, of husbands from wives, of parents from children—if a man threatens to run away, he is sure to be sold. Ben's mother was sold down South—to New Orleans—when he was about twenty years old.

I arrived in Canada on the 13th September, 1824.

Eluding the Slave Patrols

Francis Henderson

Among the most immediate dangers faced by runaways were the slave patrols that policed virtually every community, rural and urban, in the South. Patrollers could be either official agents of the state or volunteers from the white community, often drawn from the poorer, non-slaveholding classes. Many historians believe that the antebellum slave patrols were the forerunners of the Ku Klux Klan that emerged during the period of Reconstruction after the Civil War.

The duties of the slave patrols were multiple. They were charged not only with policing against slave insurrections and apprehending runaways, but also with enforcing the system of passes, without which a slave was not allowed off his or her owner's property, and with breaking up unauthorized, even informal meetings among bondsmen and women. Slave patrols functioned as a paramilitary vigilante force whose very presence was designed to provoke fear and obedience. The following selection, from Boston abolitionist Benjamin Drew's interview with ex-slave Francis Henderson, describes both the harshness of slave existence and the terror wrought by the slave patrols. In one instance recounted by Henderson, patrollers even attacked a free black man for no reason other than his race.

I escaped from slavery in Washington City, D.C., in 1841, aged nineteen. I was not sent to school when a boy, and

Benjamin Drew, *A North-Side View of Slavery. The Refugee; or The Narratives of Fugitive Slaves in Canada Related by Themselves*. Boston: John P. Jewett and Company, 1856.

had no educational advantages at all. My master's family were Church of England people themselves and wished me to attend there. I do not know my age, but suppose thirty-three.

I worked on a plantation from about ten years old till my escape. They raised wheat, corn, tobacco, and vegetables,—about forty slaves on the place. My father was a mulatto, my mother dark; they had thirteen children, of whom I was the only son. On that plantation the mulattoes were more despised than the whole blood blacks. I often wished from the fact of my condition that I had been darker. My sisters suffered from the same cause. I could frequently hear the mistress say to them, "you yellow hussy! you yellow wench!" etc. The language to me generally was, "go do so and so." But if a hoe-handle were broken or any thing went wrong, it would be every sort of a wicked expression—so bad I do not like to say what—very profane and coarse.

A Life of Hardship

Our houses were but log huts—the tops partly open—ground floor—rain would come through. My aunt was quite an old woman and had been sick several years: in rains I have seen her moving about from one part of the house to the other and rolling her bedclothes about to try to keep dry—every thing would be dirty and muddy. I lived in the house with my aunt. My bed and bedstead consisted of a board wide enough to sleep on—one end on a stool, the other placed near the fire. My pillow consisted of my jacket, my covering was whatever I could get. My bedtick was the board itself. And this was the way the single men slept, but we were comfortable in this way of sleeping, *being used to it.* I only remember having but one blanket from my owners up to the age of 19, when I ran away.

Our allowance was given weekly—a peck of sifted corn meal, a dozen and a half herrings, two and a half pounds of pork. Some of the boys would eat this up in three days, then they had to steal, or they could not perform their daily tasks. They would visit the hog-pen, sheep-pen, and granaries. I do not remember one slave but who stole some things—they

were driven to it as a matter of necessity. I myself did this—
many a time have I, with others, run among the stumps in
chase of a sheep, that we might have something to eat. If

"Follow the Drinking Gourd"

*Because slaves were generally forbidden to learn to read
and write, directions for escape routes usually circulated
by word of mouth. To minimize the risk of being overheard
instructions were often encrypted in song lyrics that might
sound innocuous to the average listener. One such song was
"Follow the Drinking Gourd." The Drinking Gourd refers
to the Big Dipper constellation. Even slaves kept deliberately ignorant of geography knew that by finding the Big
Dipper in the night sky they could locate the North Star, and
in that direction lay freedom. "Follow the Drinking Gourd"
provides coded instructions for runaways fleeing the Deep
South states of Alabama and Mississippi. The "old man"
referred to in the lyrics was an actual person, a traveling
carpenter known as "Peg Leg Joe," who passed along to
fugitives additional directions for a safe route to the North.*

When the sun comes back
And the first quail calls
Follow the drinking gourd.
For the old man is a-waiting for to carry you to freedom
If you follow the drinking gourd.

The riverbank makes a very good road.
The dead trees will show you the way.
Left foot, peg foot, traveling on,
Follow the drinking gourd.

The river ends between two hills
Follow the drinking gourd.
There's another river on the other side
Follow the drinking gourd.

When the great big river meets the little river
Follow the drinking gourd.
For the old man is a-waiting for to carry you to freedom
If you follow the drinking gourd.

colored men steal, it is because they are brought up to it. In regard to cooking, sometimes many have to cook at one fire, and before all could get to the fire to bake hoe cakes, the overseer's horn would sound: then they must go at any rate. Many a time I have gone along eating a piece of bread and meat, or herring broiled on the coals—I never sat down at a table to eat, except in harvest time, all the time I was a slave. In harvest time, the cooking is done at the great house, as the hands are wanted more in the field. This was more like people, and we liked it, for we sat down then at meals. In the summer we had one pair of linen trousers given us— nothing else; every fall, one pair of woollen pantaloons, one woollen jacket, and two cotton shirts.

Slave Drivers and Slave Patrols

My master had four sons in his family. They all left except one, who remained to be a driver. He would often come to the field and accuse the slaves of having taken so and so. If we denied it, he would whip the grown-up ones to make them own it. Many a time, when we didn't know he was anywhere round, he would be in the woods watching us— first thing we would know, he would be sitting on the fence looking down upon us, and if any had been idle, the young master would visit him with blows. I have known him to kick my aunt, an old woman who had raised and nursed him, and I have seen him punish my sisters awfully with hickories from the woods.

The slaves are watched by the patrols, who ride about to try to catch them off the quarters, especially at the house of a free person of color. I have known the slaves to stretch clothes lines across the street, high enough to let the horse pass, but not the rider; then the boys would run, and the patrols in full chase would be thrown off by running against the lines. The patrols are poor white men who live by plundering and stealing, getting rewards for runaways and setting up little shops on the public roads. They will take whatever the slaves steal, paying in money, whiskey, or whatever the slaves want. They take pigs, sheep, wheat, corn—any thing that's raised they encourage the slaves to steal; these they take to market next day. It's all speculation—all a matter of self-interest, and when the slaves run away, these same traders catch them if they can, to get the reward. If the slave threatens to expose his traffic, he does not care—for the slave's word is good for nothing—it would not be taken. There are frequent quarrels between the slaves and the poor white men. About the city on Sundays, the slaves, many of them, being fond of dress, would appear nicely clad, which seemed to provoke the poor white men. I have had them curse and damn me on this account. They would say to me, "Where are you going? Who do you belong to?" I would tell them—then, "Where did you get them clothes? I wish you belonged to me—I'd dress you up!" Then I have had them throw water on me. One time I had bought a new fur hat, and one of them threw a watermelon rind and spoiled the hat. Sometimes I have seen them throw a slave's hat on the ground and trample on it. He would pick it up, fix it as well as he could, put it on his head, and walk on. The slave had no redress but would sometimes take a petty revenge on the man's horse or saddle or something of that sort.

Common Brutalities

I knew a free man of color, who had a wife on a plantation. The patrols went to his house in the night time. He would not let them in; they broke in and beat him—nearly killed him. The next morning he went before the magistrates, bloody and dirty just as he was. All the redress he got was that he had no right to resist a white man.

An old slaveholder married into the family, who introduced a new way of whipping. He used to brag that he could pick a "nigger's" back as he would a chicken's. I went to live with him. There was one man that he used to whip every day because he was a foolish, peevish man. He would cry when the master undertook to punish him. If a man had any spirit and would say, "I am working—I am doing all I can do," he would let him alone, but there was a good deal of flogging nevertheless.

Chapter 2

Necessary
Deceptions

Chapter Preface

M ost of the popular slave narratives that were enjoyed by thousands of nineteenth-century readers recounted the ingenious ruses and equally clever disguises utilized by runaways in their treks to liberty. Henry "Box" Brown arranged to be shipped to freedom in a crate; Ellen and William Craft disguised themselves respectively as an elderly white male invalid and his faithful manservant; Moses Roper drew on his part–Native American lineage to represent himself in the Deep South as an Indian rather than an escaped black slave. Indeed, the propensity of owners to use their female slaves as sexual chattel often resulted in offspring whose mixed heritage could preclude immediate racial categorization and thus facilitate escape.

Yet most successful runaways were justifiably wary of the public roads and forms of transportations that necessitated disguising one's physical appearance. More widespread was the use of secret codes, often in such superficially innocuous songs as "Follow the Drinking Gourd" and "Swing Low, Sweet Chariot." Throughout the South state laws forbade teaching slaves to read and write, although many were either taught or taught themselves in secret. Song lyrics deflected suspicion if overheard, seeming as they did to be meaningless ditties or homespun spirituals. "Follow the Drinking Gourd," for instance, encoded a specific escape route from the Deep South, its central image a reference to the Big Dipper, whose proximity to Polaris the North Star pointed the way to freedom. Secret codes also were employed by Underground Railroad operators. Conductors and stationmasters exchanged cryptic correspondences alluding to impending or departing "freight" or "shipments" in order to confuse any potential interceptor.

An Unusual Escape

Henry "Box" Brown

The 1849 escape of Henry "Box" Brown, related in his vastly popular autobiography, was one of the most celebrated and inventive in all the slave narratives. With the assistance of a shopkeeper in Richmond, Virginia, Brown arranged to have himself shipped in a wooden crate to Philadelphia, where he was greeted by members of the local abolitionist community. Although many black abolitionists such as Frederick Douglass disapproved of former runaways publicizing the details of their escape lest future attempts by others be thwarted, Brown parlayed his unusual experience into celebrity on the antislavery lecture circuit both in the Northeast and in England where he fled after the passage of the Fugitive Slave Law. A talented artist, Brown even depicted his escape in an intricate panorama with which he toured. Although the last known reference to Brown was in 1864, when he was in England, the ingenious means of escape from slavery, from which he took his middle name, remains among the best known and most unconventional pieces of Underground Railroad lore.

I now began to get weary of my bonds; and earnestly panted after liberty. I felt convinced that I should be acting in accordance with the will of God, if I could snap in sunder those bonds by which I was held body and soul as the property of a fellow man. I looked forward to the good time which every day I more and more firmly believed would yet come, when I should walk the face of the earth in

Henry "Box" Brown, *Narrative of Henry "Box" Brown, Who Escaped from Slavery Enclosed in a Box 3 Feet Long and 2 Wide, Written from a Statement of Facts Made by Himself. With Remarks Upon the Remedy for Slavery by Charles Stearns.* Boston: Brown and Stearns, 1849.

full possession of all that freedom which the finger of God had so clearly written on the constitutions of man, and which was common to the human race; but of which, by the cruel hand of tyranny, I, and millions of my fellow-men, had been robbed.

Paying for Assistance

I was well acquainted with a storekeeper in the city of Richmond, from whom I used to purchase my provisions; and having formed a favorable opinion of his integrity, one day in the course of a little conversation with him, I said to him if I were free I would be able to do business such as he was doing; he then told me that my occupation (a tobacconist) was a money-making one, and if I were free I had no need to change for another. I then told him my circumstances in regard to my master, having to pay him 25 dollars per month, and yet that he refused to assist me in saving my wife from being sold and taken away to the South, where I should never see her again; and even refused to allow me to go and see her until my hours of labor were over. I told him this took place about five months ago, and I had been meditating my escape from slavery since, and asked him, as no person was near us, if he could give me any information about how I should proceed. I told him I had a little money and if he would assist me I would pay him for so doing. The man asked me if I was not afraid to speak that way to him; I said no, for I imagined he believed that every man had a right to liberty. He said I was quite right, and asked me how much money I would give him if he would assist me to get away. I told him that I had 166 dollars and that I would give him the half; so we ultimately agreed that I should have his service in the attempt for 86. Now I only wanted to fix upon a plan. He told me of several plans by which others had managed to effect their escape, but none of them exactly suited my taste. I then left him to think over what would be best to be done, and, in the mean time, went to consult my friend Dr. Smith, on the subject. I mentioned the plans which the storekeeper had suggested, and as he did not approve either of them very much, I still looked for some plan which would be more certain and more safe, but I was determined that come what may, I should have my freedom or die in the attempt.

A Divine Inspiration

One day, while I was at work, and my thoughts were eagerly feasting upon the idea of freedom, I felt my soul called out to heaven to breathe a prayer to Almighty God. I prayed fervently that he who seeth in secret and knew the inmost desires of my heart, would lend me his aid in bursting my fetters asunder, and in restoring me to the possession of those rights, of which men had robbed me; when the idea suddenly flashed across my mind of shutting myself *up in a box*, and getting myself conveyed as dry goods to a free state.

Being now satisfied that this was the plan for me, I went to my friend Dr. Smith and, having acquainted him with it, we agreed to have it put at once into execution not however without calculating the chances of danger with which it was attended; but buoyed up by the prospect of freedom and increased hatred to slavery I was willing to dare even death itself rather than endure any longer the clanking of those galling chains. It being still necessary to have the assistance of the storekeeper, to see that the box was kept in its right position on its passage, I then went to let him know my intention, but he said although he was willing to serve me in any way he could, he did not think I could live in a box for so long a time as would be necessary to convey me to Philadelphia, but as I had already made up my mind, he consented to accompany me and keep the box right all the way.

The Box

My next object was to procure a box, and with the assistance of a carpenter that was very soon accomplished, and taken to the place where the packing was to be performed. In the mean time the storekeeper had written to a friend in Philadelphia, but as no answer had arrived, we resolved to carry out our purpose as best we could. It was deemed necessary that I should get permission to be absent from my work for a few days, in order to keep down suspicion until I had once fairly started on the road to liberty; and as I had then a gathered finger I thought that would form a very good excuse for obtaining leave of absence; but when I showed it to one overseer, Mr. Allen, he told me it was not so bad as to prevent me from working, so with a view of making it bad enough, I got Dr. Smith to procure for me some oil of vitriol in order to drop a little of this on it, but in my hurry I dropped rather much and made it worse than there was any occasion for, in fact it was very soon eaten in to the bone, and on presenting it again to Mr. Allen I obtained the permission required, with the advice that I should go home and get a poultice of flax-meal to it, and keep it well poulticed until it got better. I took him instantly at his word and went off directly to the storekeeper who had by this time received an answer from his friend in Philadelphia, and had obtained permission to address the box to him, this friend in that city, arranging to call for it as soon as it should

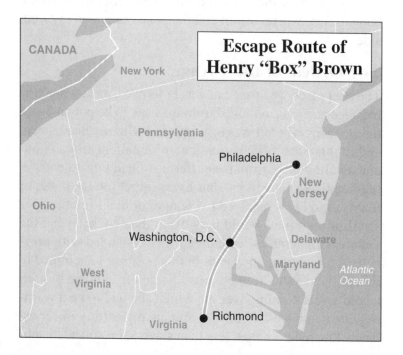

arrive. There being no time to be lost, the storekeeper, Dr. Smith, and myself, agreed to meet next morning at four o'clock, in order to get the box ready for the express train. The box which I had procured was three feet one inch wide, two feet six inches high, and two feet wide: and on the morning of the 29th day of March, 1849, I went into the box—having previously bored three gimlet holes opposite my face, for air, and provided myself with a bladder of water, both for the purpose of quenching my thirst and for wetting my face, should I feel getting faint. I took the gimlet also with me, in order that I might bore more holes if I found I had not sufficient air. Being thus equipped for the battle of liberty, my friends nailed down the lid and had me conveyed to the Express Office, which was about a mile distant from the place where I was packed. I had no sooner arrived at the office than I was turned heels up, while some person nailed something on the end of the box. I was then put upon a wagon and driven off to the depot with my head down, and I had no sooner arrived at the depot, than the man who drove the wagon tumbled me roughly into the baggage car, where, however, I happened to fall on my right side.

The Ordeal of the Voyage

The next place we arrived at was Potomac Creek, where the baggage had to be removed from the cars, to be put on board the steamer; where I was again placed with my head down, and in this dreadful position had to remain nearly an hour and a half, which, from the sufferings I had thus to endure, seemed like an age to me, but I was forgetting the battle of liberty, and I was resolved to conquer or die. I felt my eyes swelling as if they would burst from their sockets; and the veins on my temples were dreadfully distended with pressure of blood upon my head. In this position I attempted to lift my hand to my face but I had no power to move it; I felt a cold sweat coming over me which seemed to be a warning that death was about to terminate my earthly miseries, but as I feared even that, less than slavery, I resolved to submit to the will of God, and under the influence of that impression, I lifted up my soul in prayer to God, who alone, was able to deliver me. My cry was soon heard, for I could hear a man saying to another, that he had travelled a long way and had been standing there two hours, and he would like to get somewhat to sit down; so perceiving my box, standing on end, he threw it down and then two sat upon it. I was thus relieved from a state of agony which may be more easily imagined than described. I could hear the men talking, and heard one of them asking the other what he supposed *the box contained;* his companion replied he guessed it was "THE MAIL." I too thought it was a mail [punning on the homonym "male"] but not such a mail as he supposed it to be.

The next place at which we arrived was the city of Washington, where I was taken from the steam-boat, and again placed upon a wagon and carried to the depot right side up with care; but when the driver arrived at the depot I heard him call for some person to help to take the box off the wagon, and some one answered him to the effect that he might throw it off; but, says the driver, it is marked "this side up with care;" so if I throw it off I might break something, the other answered him that it did not matter if he broke all that was in it, the railway company were able enough to pay for it. No sooner were these words spoken than I began to tumble from the wagon, and falling on the end where my head was, I could hear my neck give a crack, as if it had been snapped asunder and I was knocked completely insensible. The first thing I heard after that, was some person saying, "there is no room for the box, it will have to remain and be sent through tomorrow with the luggage train"; but the Lord had not quite forsaken me, for in answer to my earnest prayer He so ordered affairs that I should not be left behind; and I now heard a man say that the box had come with the express, and it must be sent on. I was then tumbled into the car with my head downwards again, but the car had not proceeded far before, more luggage having to be taken in, my box got shifted about and so happened to turn upon its right side; and in this position I remained till I got to Philadelphia, of our arrival in which place I was informed by hearing some person say, "We are in port and at Philadelphia." My heart then leaped for joy, and I wondered if any person knew that such a box was there.

A "Resurrection"

Here it may be proper to observe that the man who had promised to accompany my box failed to do what he promised; but, to prevent it remaining long at the station after its arrival, he sent a telegraphic message to his friend, and I was only twenty seven hours in the box, though travelling a distance of three hundred and fifty miles.

I was now placed in the depot amongst the other luggage, where I lay till seven o'clock P.M., at which time a wagon drove up, and I heard a person inquire for such a box as that in which I was. I was then placed on a wagon and conveyed to the house where my friend in Richmond had arranged I should be received. A number of persons soon collected round the box after it was taken in to the house, but as I did not know what was going on I kept myself quiet. I heard a man say, "let us rap upon the box and see if he is alive;" and immediately a rap ensued and a voice said, tremblingly, "Is all right within?" to which I replied—"all right." The joy of the friends was very great; when they heard that I was alive, they soon managed to break open the box, and then came my resurrection from the grave of slavery. I rose a freeman, but I was too weak, by reason of long confinement in that box, to be able to stand, so I immediately swooned away. After my recovery from the swoon the first thing which arrested my attention was the presence of a number of friends, every one seeming more anxious than another to have an opportunity of rendering me their assistance and of bidding me a hearty welcome to the possession of my natural rights—I had risen as it were from the dead. I felt much more than I could readily express, but as the kindness of Almighty God had been so conspicuously shown in my deliverance, I burst forth into the following hymn of thanksgiving,

I waited patiently, I waited patiently for the Lord, for the Lord;
And he inclined unto me, and heard my calling:
I waited patiently, I waited patiently for the Lord,
And he inclined unto me, and heard my calling:
And he hath put a new song in my mouth,
Even a thanksgiving, even a thanksgiving, even a thanksgiving
    unto our God.

A Secret Hiding Place

Harriet Jacobs

Harriet Jacobs's memoir *Incidents in the Life of a Slave Girl* (published under the pseudonym Linda Brent) was published in 1861, the same year as the outbreak of the Civil War. Yet the story told by Jacobs, a former North Carolina slave, is among the most remarkable of the genre for its candid description of the sexual abuse all too commonly inflicted upon slave women by white owners. Jacobs's escape from her tormenter Dr. James Norcom was also distinctive, as she took refuge in her grandmother's shed, where she hid for seven years before at last fleeing to New York City. Once in the North, Jacobs became involved in the antislavery movement. She was befriended by the Quaker abolitionist Lydia Maria Child, who encouraged Jacobs to compose her memoir and helped with its editing. Although Jacobs was literate, for many years readers and scholars often mistakenly assumed that Child was the primary author of *Incidents in the Life of a Slave Girl.*

Despite its striking frankness, Jacobs's narrative draws on the conventions of sentimental novels widely popular among nineteenth-century female readers. The memoir emphasizes slavery's harsh toll on cherished Victorian principles of female chastity and maternal feelings (Jacobs had two children by a free white man). The following selection describes Jacobs's seven-year ordeal hiding in her grandmother's attic from Dr. Norcom (in the memoir called "Dr. Flint") and her ultimate decision—and nerve-wracking plans—to escape aboard a northern-bound ship. Unlike many fugitive slave narratives written by men, Jacobs's stresses the strong family

Harriet Jacobs, *Incidents in the Life of a Slave Girl, Seven Years Concealed,* edited by Lydia Maria Child. Boston: Harriet Jacobs, 1861.

bonds that sustained her in hiding and supported her in escape. By underscoring a "feminine" perspective Jacobs was reminding a largely white, female readership of values shared by all women regardless of the color of their skin.

A small shed had been added to my grandmother's house years ago. Some boards were laid across the joists at the top, and between these boards and the roof was a very small garret never occupied by any thing but rats and mice. It was a pent roof, covered with nothing but shingles, according to the southern custom for such buildings. The garret was only nine feet long and seven wide. The highest part was three feet high, and sloped down abruptly to the loose board floor. There was no admission for either light or air. My uncle Philip, who was a carpenter, had very skilfully made a concealed trap-door, which communicated with the storeroom. He had been doing this while I was waiting in the swamp. The storeroom opened upon a piazza. To this hole I was conveyed as soon as I entered the house. The air was stifling; the darkness total. A bed had been spread on the floor. I could sleep quite comfortably on one side; but the slope was so sudden that I could not turn on the other without hitting the roof. The rats and mice ran over my bed; but I was weary, and I slept such sleep as the wretched may, when a tempest has passed over them. Morning came. I knew it only by the noises I heard; for in my small den day and night were all the same. I suffered for air even more than for light. But I was not comfortless. I heard the voices of my children. There was joy and there was sadness in the sound. It made my tears flow. How I longed to speak to them! I was eager to look on their faces; but there was no hole, no crack, through which I could peep. This continued darkness was oppressive. It seemed horrible to sit or lie in a cramped position day after day, without one gleam of light. Yet I would have chosen this, rather than my lot as a slave, though white people considered it an easy one; and it was so compared with the fate of others. I was never cruelly overworked; I was never lacerated with the whip from head to foot; I was never so beaten and bruised that I could not turn from one side to the other; I never had my heel-strings cut to prevent my running away; I was never chained to a log and forced to drag it about, while I toiled in the fields from morning till night; I was never branded with hot iron, or torn by bloodhounds. On the contrary, I had always been kindly treated, and tenderly cared for, until I came into the hands of Dr. Flint. I had never wished for freedom till then. But though my life in slavery was comparatively devoid of hardships, God pity the woman who is compelled to lead such a life!

Adjusting to Confinement

My food was passed up to me through the trap-door my uncle had contrived; and my grandmother, my uncle Phillip, and aunt Nancy would seize such opportunities as they could, to mount up there and chat with me at the opening. But of course this was not safe in the daytime. It must all be done in darkness. It was impossible for me to move in an erect position, but I crawled about my den for exercise. One day I hit my head against something, and found it was a gimlet [a boring tool]. My uncle had left it sticking there when he made the trap-door. I was as rejoiced as Robinson Crusoe could have been at finding such a treasure. It put a lucky thought into my head. I said to myself, "Now I will have some light. Now I will see my children." I did not dare to begin my work during the daytime, for fear of attracting attention. But I groped round; and having found the side next the street, where I could frequently see my children, I stuck the gimlet in and waited for evening, I bored three rows of holes, one above another; then I bored out the interstices between. I thus succeeded in making one hole about an inch long and an inch broad. I sat by it till late into the night, to enjoy the little whiff of air that floated in. In the morning I watched for my children. The first person I saw in the street was Dr. Flint. I had a shuddering, superstitious feeling that it was a bad omen. Several familiar faces passed by. At last I heard the merry laugh of children, and presently two sweet little faces were looking up at me, as though they knew I was there, and were conscious of the joy they imparted. How I longed to tell them I was there!

My condition was now a little improved. But for weeks I was tormented by hundreds of little red insects, fine as a needle's point, that pierced through my skin, and produced an intolerable burning. The good grandmother gave me herb teas and cooling medicines, and finally I got rid of them. The heat of my den was intense, for nothing but thin shingles protected me from the scorching summer's sun. But I had my consolations. Through my peeping-hole I could watch the children, and when they were near enough, I could hear their talk. Aunt Nancy brought me all the news she could hear at Dr. Flint's. From her I learned that the doctor had written to New York to a colored woman, who had been born and raised in our neighborhood, and had breathed his contaminating atmosphere. He offered her a reward if she could find out any thing about me. I know not what was the nature of her reply; but he soon after started for New York in haste, saying to his family that he had business of importance to transact. I peeped at him as he passed on his way to the steamboat. It was a satisfaction to have miles of land and water between us, even for a little while; and it was a still greater satisfaction to know that he believed me to be in the Free States. My little den seemed less dreary than it had done. He returned, as he did from his former journey to New York, without obtaining any satisfactory information. When he passed our house next morning, Benny was standing at the gate. He had heard them say that he had gone to find me, and he called out, "Dr. Flint, did you bring my mother home? I want to see her." The doctor stamped his foot at him in a rage, and exclaimed, "Get out of the way, you little damned rascal! If you don't, I'll cut off your head."

Benny ran terrified into the house, saying, "You can't put me in jail again. I don't belong to you now." It was well that the wind carried the words away from the doctor's ear. I told my grandmother of it, when we had our next conference at the trap-door; and begged of her not to allow the children to be impertinent to the irascible old man.

The Search Continues

Autumn came, with a pleasant abatement of heat. My eyes had become accustomed to the dim light, and by holding my book or work in a certain position near the aperture I contrived to read and sew. That was a great relief to the tedious monotony of my life. But when winter came, the cold penetrated through the thin shingle roof, and I was dreadfully chilled. The winters there are not so long, or so severe, as in northern latitudes; but the houses are not built to shelter from cold, and my little den was peculiarly comfortless. The kind grandmother brought me bedclothes and warm drinks. Often I was obliged to lie in bed all day to keep comfortable; but with all my precautions, my shoulders and feet were frostbitten. O, those long, gloomy days, with no object for my eye to rest upon, and no thoughts to occupy my mind, except the dreary past and the uncertain future! I was thankful when there came a day sufficiently mild for me to wrap myself up and sit at the loophole to watch the passers by. Southerners have the habit of stopping and talking in the streets, and I heard many conversations not intended to meet my ears. I heard slave-hunters planning how to catch some poor fugitive. Several times I heard allusions to Dr. Flint, myself, and the history of my children, who, perhaps, were playing near the gate. One would say, "I wouldn't move my little finger to catch her, as old Flint's property." Another would say, "I'll catch any nigger for the reward. A man ought to have what belongs to him, if he is a damned brute." The opinion was often expressed that I was in the Free States. Very rarely did any one suggest that I might be in the vicinity. Had the least suspicion rested on my grandmother's house, it would have been burned to the ground. But it was the last place they thought of. Yet there was no place, where slavery existed, that could have afforded me so good a place of concealment.

Dr. Flint and his family repeatedly tried to coax and bribe

my children to tell something they had heard said about me. One day the doctor took them into a shop, and offered them some bright little silver pieces and gay handkerchiefs if they would tell where their mother was. Ellen shrank away from him, and would not speak; but Benny spoke up, and said, "Dr. Flint, I don't know where my mother is. I guess she's in New York; and when you go there again, I wish you'd ask her to come home, for I want to see her; but if you put her in jail, or tell her you'll cut her head off, I'll tell her to go right back.". . .

Preparing to Escape

I hardly expect that the reader will credit me, when I affirm that I lived in that little dismal hole, almost deprived of light and air, and with no space to move my limbs, for nearly seven years. But it is a fact; and to me a sad one, even now; for my body still suffers from the effects of that long imprisonment, to say nothing of my soul. Members of my family, now living in New York and Boston, can testify to the truth of what I say.

Countless were the nights that I sat late at the little loophole scarcely large enough to give me a glimpse of one twinkling star. There, I heard the patrols and slave-hunters conferring together about the capture of runaways, well knowing how rejoiced they would be to catch me.

Season after season, year after year, I peeped at my children's faces, and heard their sweet voices, with a heart yearning all the while to say, "Your mother is here." Sometimes it appeared to me as if ages had rolled away since I entered upon that gloomy, monotonous existence. At times, I was stupefied and listless; at other times I became very impatient to know when these dark years would end, and I should again be allowed to feel the sunshine, and breathe the pure air.

Thoughts of the North

After Ellen left us, this feeling increased. Mr. Sands had agreed that Benny might go to the north whenever his uncle

Phillip could go with him; and I was anxious to be there also, to watch over my children, and protect them so far as I was able. Moreover, I was likely to be drowned out of my den, if I remained much longer; for the slight roof was getting badly out of repair, and uncle Phillip was afraid to remove the shingles, lest some one should get a glimpse of me. When storms occurred in the night, they spread mats and bits of carpet, which in the morning appeared to have been laid out to dry; but to cover the roof in the daytime might have attracted attention. Consequently, my clothes and bedding were often drenched; a process by which the pains and aches in my cramped and stiffened limbs were greatly increased. I revolved various plans of escape in my mind, which I sometimes imparted to my grandmother, when she came to whisper with me at the trap-door. The kind-hearted old woman had an intense sympathy for runaways. She had known too much of the cruelties inflicted on those who were captured. Her memory always flew back at once to the sufferings of her bright and handsome son, Benjamin, the youngest and dearest of her flock. So, whenever I alluded to the subject, she would groan out, "O, don't think of it, child. You'll break my heart." I had no good old aunt Nancy now to encourage me; but my brother William and my children were continually beckoning me to the north.

And now I must go back a few months in my story. I have stated that the first of January was the time for selling slaves, or leasing them out to new masters. If time were counted by heart-throbs, the poor slaves might reckon years of suffering during that festival so joyous to the free. On the New Year's day preceding my aunt's death, one of my friends, named Fanny, was to be sold at auction, to pay her master's debts. My thoughts were with her during all the day, and at night I anxiously inquired what had been her fate. I was told that she had been sold to one master, and her four little girls to another master, far distant; that she had escaped from her purchaser, and was not to be found. Her mother was the old Aggie I have spoken of. She lived in a small tenement belonging to my grandmother, and built on the same lot with her own house. Her dwelling was searched and watched, and that brought the patrols so near me that I was obliged to keep very close in my den. The hunters were somehow eluded; and not long afterwards Benny accidentally caught sight of Fanny in her mother's hut. He told his grandmother, who charged him never to speak of it, explaining to him the frightful consequences; and he never betrayed the trust. Aggie little dreamed that my grandmother knew where her daughter was concealed, and that the stooping form of her old neighbor was bending under a similar burden of anxiety and fear; but these dangerous secrets deepened the sympathy between the two old persecuted mothers.

A Chance for Freedom

My friend Fanny and I remained many weeks hidden within call of each other; but she was unconscious of the fact. I longed to have her share my den, which seemed a more secure retreat than her own; but I had brought so much trouble on my grandmother that it seemed wrong to ask her to incur greater risks. My restlessness increased. I had lived too long in bodily pain and anguish of spirit. Always I was in dread that by some accident, or some contrivance, slavery would succeed in snatching my children from me. This thought drove me nearly frantic, and I determined to steer for the North Star at all hazards. At this crisis, Providence opened an unexpected way for me to escape. My friend Peter came one evening, and asked to speak with me. "Your day has come, Linda," said he. "I have found a chance for you to go to the Free States. You have a fortnight to decide." The news seemed too good to be true; but Peter explained his arrangements and told me all that was necessary was for me to say I would go. I was going to answer him with a joyful yes, when the thought of Benny came to my mind. I told him the temptation was exceedingly strong, but I was terribly afraid of Dr. Flint's alleged power over my child, and that I could not go and leave him behind. Peter remonstrated earnestly. He said such a good chance might never occur again; that Benny was free and could be sent to me; and that for the sake of my children's welfare I ought not to hesitate a moment. I told him I would consult with uncle Phillip. My uncle rejoiced in the plan, and bade me go by all means. He promised, if his life was spared, that he would either bring or send my son to me as soon as I reached a place of safety. I resolved to go, but thought nothing had better be said to my grandmother till very near the time of departure. But my uncle thought she would feel it more keenly if I left here so suddenly. "I will reason with her," said he, "and convince her how necessary it is, not only for your sake, but for hers also. You cannot be blind to the fact that she is sinking under her burdens." I was not blind to it. I knew that my concealment was an ever-present source of anxiety, and that the older she grew the more nervously fearful she was of discovery. My uncle talked with her, and finally succeeded in persuading her that it was absolutely necessary for me to seize the chance so unexpectedly offered.

The anticipation of being a free woman proved almost too much for my weak frame. The excitement stimulated me and at the same time bewildered me. I made busy preparations for my journey, and for my son to follow me. I resolved to have an interview with him before I went, that I might give him cautions and advice and tell him how anxiously I should be waiting for him at the north. Grandmother stole up to me as often as possible to whisper words of counsel. She insisted upon my writing to Dr. Flint, as soon as I arrived in the Free States, and asking him to sell me to her. She said she would sacrifice her house and all she had in the world for the sake of having me safe with my children in any part of the world. If she could only live to know that she could die in peace. I promised the dear old faithful friend that I would write to her as soon as I arrived, and put the letter in a safe way to reach her; but in my own mind I resolved that not another cent of her hard earnings should be spent to pay rapacious slaveholders for what they called their property. And even if I had not been unwilling to buy what I had already a right to possess, common humanity would have prevented me from accepting the generous of-

fer, at the expense of turning my aged relative out of house
and home when she was trembling on the brink of the grave.

Doubts and Fears

I was to escape in a vessel; but I forbear to mention any further particulars. I was in readiness, but the vessel was unexpectedly detained several days. Meantime, news came to
town of a most horrible murder committed on a fugitive
slave named James. Charity, the mother of this unfortunate
young man, had been an old acquaintance of ours. I have
told the shocking particulars of his death in my description
of some of the neighboring slaveholders. My grandmother,
always nervously sensitive about runaways, was terribly
frightened. She felt sure that a similar fate awaited me if I
did not desist from my enterprise. She sobbed and groaned
and entreated me not to go. Her excessive fear was somewhat contagious, and my heart was not proof against her extreme agony. I was grievously disappointed, but I promised
to relinquish my project.

When my friend Peter was apprised of this, he was both
disappointed and vexed. He said that, judging from our past
experience, it would be a long time before I had such another chance to throw away. I told him it need not be thrown
away; that I had a friend concealed near by who would be
glad enough to take the place that had been provided for me.
I told him about poor Fanny, and the kind-hearted, noble fellow, who never turned his back upon any body in distress,
white or black, expressed his readiness to help her. Aggie
was much surprised when she found that we knew her secret. She was rejoiced to hear of such a chance for Fanny,
and arrangements were made for her to go on board the vessel the next night. They both supposed that I had long been
at the north, therefore my name was not mentioned in the
transaction. Fanny was carried on board at the appointed
time and stowed away in a very small cabin. This accom-
modation had been purchased at a price that would pay for
a voyage to England. But when one proposes to go to fine
old England, they stop to calculate whether they can afford

the cost of the pleasure; while in making a bargain to escape from slavery, the trembling victim is ready to say, "take all I have, only don't betray me!"

The next morning I peeped through my loophole, and saw that it was dark and cloudly. At night I received news that the wind was ahead, and the vessel had not sailed. I was exceedingly anxious about Fanny, and Peter, too, who was running a tremendous risk at my instigation. Next day the wind and weather remained the same. Poor Fanny had been half dead with fright when they carried her on board, and I could readily imagine how she must be suffering now. Grandmother came often to my den to say how thankful she was I did not go. On the third morning she rapped for me to come down to the storeroom. The poor old sufferer was breaking down under her weight of trouble. She was easily flurried now. I found her in a nervous, excited state, but I was not aware that she had forgotten to lock the door behind her as usual. She was exceedingly worried about the detention of the vessel. She was afraid all would be discovered, and then Fanny, and Peter, and I, would all be tortured to death, and Phillip would be utterly ruined, and her house would be torn down. Poor Peter! If he should die such a horrible death as the poor slave James had lately done, and all for his kindness in trying to help me, how dreadful it would be for us all! Alas, the thought was familiar to me and had sent many a sharp pang through my heart. I tried to suppress my own anxiety and speak soothingly to her. She brought in some allusion to aunt Nancy, the dear daughter she had recently buried, and then she lost all control of herself. As she stood there, trembling and sobbing, a voice from the piazza called out, "Whar is you, aunt Marthy?" Grandmother was startled, and in her agitation opened the door, without thinking of me. In stepped Jenny, the mischievous housemaid, who had tried to enter my room, when I was concealed in the house of my white benefactress. "I's bin huntin ebery whar for you, aunt Marthy," said she. "My missis wants you to send her some crackers." I had slunk down behind a barrel, which entirely screened me, but I imagined that Jenny was looking directly at the spot, and my heart beat violently. My grandmother immediately thought [of] what she had done, and went out quickly with Jenny to count the crackers locking the door after her. She returned to me in a few minutes, the perfect picture of despair. "Poor child!" she exclaimed, "my carelessness has ruined you. The boat ain't gone yet. Get ready immediately and go with Fanny. I ain't got another word to say against it now; for there's no telling what may happen this day."

A Last-Minute Passenger

Uncle Phillip was sent for, and he agreed with his mother in thinking that Jenny would inform Dr. Flint in less than twenty-four hours. He advised getting me on board the boat, if possible; if not, I had better keep very still in my den where they could not find me without tearing the house down. He said it would not do for him to move in the matter because suspicion would be immediately excited; but he promised to communicate with Peter. I felt reluctant to apply to him again, having implicated him too much already; but there seemed to be no alternative. Vexed as Peter had been by my indecision, he was true to his generous nature and said at once that he would do his best to help me, trusting I should show myself a stronger woman this time.

He immediately proceeded to the wharf and found that the wind had shifted, and the vessel was slowly beating down stream. On some pretext of urgent necessity, he offered two boatmen a dollar apiece to catch up with her. He was of lighter complexion than the boatmen he hired, and when the captain saw them coming so rapidly, he thought officers were pursuing his vessel in search of the runaway slave he had on board. They hoisted sails, but the boat gained upon them, and the indefatigable Peter sprang on board.

The captain at once recognized him. Peter asked him to go below to speak about a bad bill he had given him. When he told his errand, the captain replied, "Why, the woman's here already; and I've put her where you or the devil would have a tough job to find her."

"But it is another woman I want to bring," said Peter. "She is in great distress, too, and you shall be paid any thing within reason, if you'll stop and take her."

"What's her name?" inquired the captain.

"Linda," he replied.

"That's the name of the woman already here," rejoined the captain. "By George! I believe you mean to betray me."

"O!" exclaimed Peter, "God knows I wouldn't harm a hair of your head. I am too grateful to you. But there really is another woman in great danger. Do have the humanity to stop and take her!"

After a while they came to an understanding. Fanny, not dreaming I was any where about in that region, had assumed my name, though she called herself Johnson. "Linda is a common name," said Peter, "and the woman I want to bring is Linda Brent."

The captain agreed to wait at a certain place till evening, being handsomely paid for his detention.

Of course, the day was an anxious one for us all. But we concluded that if Jenny had seen me, she would be too wise to let her mistress know of it; and that she probably would not get a chance to see Dr. Flint's family till evening, for I knew very well what were the rules in that household. I afterwards believed that she did not see me; for nothing ever came of it, and she was one of those base characters that would have jumped to betray a suffering fellow being for the sake of thirty pieces of silver.

A Bittersweet Good-Bye

I made all my arrangements to go on board as soon as it was dusk. The intervening time I resolved to spend with my son. I had not spoken to him for seven years, though I had been under the same roof, and seen him every day when I was well enough to sit at the loophole. I did not dare to venture beyond the storeroom; so they brought him there and locked us up together in a place concealed from the piazza door. It was an agitating interview for both of us. After we had talked and wept together for a little while, he said, "Mother,

I'm glad you're going away. I wish I could go with you. I knew you was here; and I have been so afraid they would come and catch you!"

I was greatly surprised and asked him how he had found it out.

He replied, "I was standing under the eaves, one day, before Ellen went away, and I heard somebody cough up over the wood shed. I don't know what made me think it was you, but I did think so. I missed Ellen, the night before she went away; and grandmother brought her back into the room in the night; and I thought maybe she'd been to see you, before she went, for I heard grandmother whisper to her, 'Now go to sleep; and remember never to tell.'"

I asked him if he ever mentioned his suspicions to his sister. He said he never did; but after he heard the cough, if he saw her playing with other children on that side of the house, he always tried to coax her round to the other side, for fear they would hear me cough, too. He said he had kept a close lookout for Dr. Flint, and if he saw him speak to a constable, or a patrol, he always told grandmother. I now recollected that I had seen him manifest uneasiness when people were on that side of the house, and I had at the time been puzzled to conjecture a motive for his actions. Such prudence may seem extraordinary in a boy of twelve years, but slaves, being surrounded by mysteries, deceptions, and dangers, early learn to be suspicious and watchful and prematurely cautious and cunning. He had never asked a question of grandmother, or uncle Phillip, and I had often heard him chime in with other children when they spoke of my being at the north.

Trust in God

I told him I was now really going to the Free States, and if he was a good, honest boy, and a loving child to his dear old grandmother, the Lord would bless him, and bring him to me, and we and Ellen would live together. He began to tell me that grandmother had not eaten any thing all day. While he was speaking, the door was unlocked, and she came in with a small ball of money which she wanted me to take. I begged her to keep a part of it, at least, to pay for Benny's being sent to the north; but she insisted, while her tears were falling fast, that I should take the whole. "You may be sick among strangers," she said, "and they would send you to the poorhouse to die." Ah, that good grandmother!

For the last time I went up to my nook. Its desolate appearance no longer chilled me, for the light of hope had risen in my soul. Yet, even with the blessed prospect of freedom before me, I felt very sad at leaving forever that old homestead where I had been sheltered so long by the dear old grandmother; where I had dreamed my first young dream of love; and where, after that had faded away, my children came to twine themselves so closely round my desolate heart. As the hour approached for me to leave, I again descended to the storeroom. My grandmother and Benny were there. She took me by the hand and said, "Linda, let us pray." We knelt down together, with my child pressed to my heart, and my other arm round the faithful, loving old friend I was about to leave forever. On no other occasion has it ever been my lot to listen to so fervent a supplication for mercy and protection, it thrilled through my heart and inspired me with trust in God.

Peter was waiting for me in the street. I was soon by his side, faint in body, but strong of purpose. I did not look back upon the old place, though I felt that I should never see it again.

A Lie That Leads to Freedom

Moses Roper

Like Frederick Douglass and William Wells Brown after him, eminent black abolitionist and onetime fugitive Moses Roper found refuge and a receptive audience in England when fear of capture led him to leave the American Northeast. The son of an African-Indian house slave and the white planter who owned her, Roper was born in Caswell County, North Carolina, but spent his early life across the South under several different masters. Roper's many failed attempts at escape resulted in brutal punishment culminating in his sale or exchange into still harsher circumstances. Undaunted, Roper, at last succeeded in fleeing bondage in 1833, securing papers allowing him to attain a job as a steward on a ship bound for New York. He worked at odd jobs throughout the Northeast, and joined Boston's American Anti-Slavery Society. The frequent advertisements for his capture prompted Roper to sail for England at the end of 1835, but he continued his involvement with the antislavery movement. British abolitionists came to Roper's aid, helping him to receive a formal education. By 1837 Roper had established himself on the British abolitionist lecture circuit, his reputation secured by the appearance of his memoirs, which were also published in Philadelphia. In 1844 Roper, his English wife, and first child resettled in Canada.

In the following selection excerpted from his memoirs, Roper describes his final, successful escape from slavery, an escape especially arduous because his point of departure is

Moses Roper, *A Narrative of the Adventures and Escape of Moses Roper from American Slavery*. Philadelphia: Merrihew & Gunn, 1838.

the Deep South, not a border state with potential haven only a
river crossing away. Roper relies greatly on his wits as he
convinces those he encounters that he is legitimately bound
for Augusta, Georgia, and has lost his passport. He takes
advantage of his mixed racial background to pass as a Native
American rather than a black man. Yet even as he is safely
aboard a New York–bound ship, Roper realizes that the dangers facing a runaway slave are far from behind him.

In the year 1834, Mr. Beveridge [Roper's current owner],
who was now residing in Appalachicola, a town in West
Florida, became a bankrupt, when all his property was sold,
and I fell into the hands of a very cruel master, Mr. Register, a planter in the same state, of whom, knowing his sav-
age character, I always had a dread. Previously to his pur-
chasing me, he had frequently taunted me, by saying, "You
have been a gentleman long enough, and, whatever may be
the consequences, I intend to buy you." To which I remarked, that I would on no account live with him if I could
help it. Nevertheless, intent upon his purpose, in the month
of July, 1834, he bought me, after which, I was so exasper-
ated that I cared not whether I lived or died; in fact, whilst
I was on my passage from Appalachicola, I procured a quart
bottle of whiskey for the purpose of so intoxicating myself
that I might be able either to plunge myself into the river or
so to enrage my master that he should dispatch me forthwith. I was, however, by a kind Providence, prevented from
committing this horrid deed by an old slave on board who,
knowing my intention, secretly took the bottle from me; after which my hands were tied, and I was led into the town
of Ochesa to a warehouse where my master was asked by
the proprietor of the place the reason for his confining my
hands; in answer to which, Mr. Register said that he had
purchased me. The proprietor, however, persuaded him to
untie me; after which my master, being excessively drunk,
asked for a cow-hide, intending to flog me, from which the
proprietor dissuaded him, saying that he had known me for

some time, and he was sure that I did not require to be flogged. From this place, we proceeded about mid-day on our way, he placing me on the bare back of a half starved old horse which he had purchased, and upon which sharp surface he kindly intended I should ride about eighty miles, the distance we were then from his home. In this unpleasant situation, I could not help reflecting upon the prospects before me, not forgetting that I had heard that my new master had been in the habit of stealing cattle and other property, and among other things, a slave woman, and that I had said, as it afterwards turned out, in the hearing of some one who communicated the saying to my master, that I had been accustomed to live with a gentleman and not with a rogue; and, finding that he had been informed of this, I had the additional dread of a few hundred lashes for it on my arrival at my destination.

A Necessary Lie

About two hours after we started, it began to rain very heavily and continued to do so until we arrived at Marianna, about twelve at night, where we were to rest till morning. My master here questioned me as to whether I intended to run away or not; and I, not then knowing the sin of lying, at once told him that I would not. He then gave me his clothes to dry; I took them to the kitchen for that purpose, and he retired to bed, taking a bag of clothes belonging to me with him as a kind of security, I presume, for my safety. In an hour or two afterwards, I took his clothes to him dried and found him fast asleep. I placed them by his side and said that I would then take my own to dry too, taking care to speak loud enough to ascertain whether he was asleep or not, knowing that he had a dirk and a pistol by his side, which he would not have hesitated using against me if I had attempted secretly to have procured them. I was glad to find that the effects of his drinking the day before had caused his sleeping very soundly, and I immediately resolved on making my escape; and without loss of time, started with my few clothes into the woods, which were in the immediate neighbourhood; and, after running many miles, I came to the river Chapoli, which is very deep, and so beset with alligators that I dared not attempt to swim across. I paced up and down this river, with the hope of finding a conveyance across, for a whole day, the succeeding night, and till noon the following day, which was Saturday. About twelve o'-clock on that day I discovered an Indian canoe, which had not, from all appearance, been used for some time; this, of course, I used to convey myself across, and after being obliged to go a little way down the river, by means of a

Masks of Docility

For many slaves, deception and dissembling were a way of life on the plantation. Aware of harsh punishments for even the hint of insubordination, slaves sometimes chose to pretend to be the contented, agreeable "Sambos" that proslavery propaganda extolled in defense of the institution, as Ronald Takaki points out in the following excerpt. But Takaki also reminds his readers that affecting childlike affability could be more than merely a coping strategy for slaves. Such feigning could and frequently did serve to deflect an owner's suspicion and thus facilitate a slave's escape.

But slaves who behaved like Sambos might not have actually been Sambos: they might have been playing the role of loyal and congenial slaves in order to get favors or to survive, while keeping their inner selves hidden. Masters themselves sometimes had difficulty determining a slave's true personality. "So deceitful is the Negro," a master explained, "that as far as my own experience extends I could never in a single instance decipher his character. . . . We planters could never get at the truth." For many slaves, illusion protected them from their masters. "The only weapon of self defence that I could use successfully, was that of deception," explained fugitive slave Henry Bibb. Another former slave explained that one had to "know the *heart* of the poor slave—learn his secret thoughts—thoughts he dare not utter in the hearing of the white man."

piece of wood I providentially found in the boat, I landed on the opposite side. Here I found myself surrounded by planters looking for me, in consequence of which I hid myself in the bushes until night, when I again travelled several miles to the farm of a Mr. Robinson, a large sugar-planter, where I rested till morning in a field. Afterwards I set out, working my way through the woods about twenty miles towards the east; this I knew by my knowledge of the position of the sun at its rising. Having reached the Chattahoochee River, which divides Florida from Georgia, I was again puz-

Indeed, many slaves wore masks of docility and deference in order to shroud subversive plans. Every year thousands of slaves became fugitives, making their way north to freedom, and many of these runaways had seemed passive and cheerful before they escaped. . . .

After his flight north, fugitive J.W. Loguen received a letter from his former owner. "You know that we reared you as we reared our own children," wrote Mrs. Sarah Logue; "that you was never abused, and that shortly before you ran away, when your master asked you if you would like to be sold, you said you would not leave him to go with any body." In his reply, Loguen caustically remarked: "Woman, did you raise your *own children* for the market? Did you raise them for the whipping-post?" The ex-slave boldly proclaimed his love for liberty: "Wretched woman! Be it known to you that I value my freedom . . . more, indeed, than my own life; more than all the lives of all the slaveholders and tyrants under heaven."

Sometimes a slave would play the role of Sambo and then strike directly at his tyrant. Slavemaster William Pearce told one of his erring slaves that he would be whipped after supper. When the slave was called out, he approached Pearce submissively. As soon as he was within striking distance, the slave pulled out a concealed ax and split his master's head.

Ronald Takaki, *A Different Mirror: A History of Multicultural America.* New York: Little, Brown, 1993.

zled to know how to cross. It was three o'clock in the day when a number of persons were fishing; having walked for some hours along the banks, I at last, after dark, procured a ferry-boat, which not being able, from the swiftness of the river, to steer direct across, I was carried many miles down the river, landing on the Georgian side, from whence I proceeded on through the woods two or three miles and came to a little farm-house about twelve at night; at a short distance from the house, I found an old slave hut, into which I went, and informed the old man, who appeared seventy or eighty years old, that I had had a very bad master, from whom I had run away; and asked him if he could give me something to eat, having had no suitable food for three or four days; he told me he had nothing but a piece of dry Indian bread, which he cheerfully gave me; having eaten it, I went on a short distance from the hut and laid down in the wood to rest for an hour or two.

All the following day (Monday), I continued travelling through the woods, was greatly distressed for want of water to quench my thirst, it being a very dry country, till I came to Spring Creek, which is a wide, deep stream, and with some of which I gladly quenched my thirst. I then proceeded to cross the same by a bridge close by, and continued my way till dusk. I came to a gentleman's house in the woods, where I inquired how far it was to the next house, taking care to watch an opportunity to ask some individual whom I could master, and get away from, if any interruption to my progress was attempted. I went on for some time, it being a very fine moonlight night, and was presently alarmed by the howling of a wolf very near me, which I concluded was calling other wolves to join him in attacking me, having understood that they always assemble in numbers for such a purpose. The howling increased, and I was still pursued, and the numbers were evidently increasing fast; but I was happily rescued from my dreadful fright by coming to some cattle, which attracted the wolves and saved my life; for I could not get up the trees for safety, they being very tall pines, the lowest branches of which were at least forty or fifty feet from the ground, and the trunks very large and smooth.

About two o'clock I came to the house of a Mr. Cherry on the borders of the Flint River; I went up to the house, and called them up to beg something to eat; but having nothing cooked, they kindly allowed me to lie down in the porch, where they made me a bed. In conversation with this Mr. Cherry, I discovered that I had known him before, having been in a steamboat, the *Versailles*, some months previous, which sunk very near his house, but which I did not at first discern to be the same. I then thought that it would not be prudent for me to stop there, and therefore told them I was in a hurry to get on and must start very early again, he having no idea who I was; and I gave his son six cents to take me across the river, which he did when the sun was about half an hour high, and unfortunately landed me where there was a man building a boat, who knew me very well, and my former master too; he calling me by name, asked me where I was going.

I was very much frightened at being discovered, but summoned up courage, and said, that my master had gone on to Tallyhassa by the coach, and that there was not room for me, and I had to walk round to meet him. I then asked the man to put me into the best road to get there, which, however, I knew as well as he did, having travelled there before; he directed me the best way, but I of course took the contrary direction, wanting to get on to Savannah. By this hasty and wicked deception I saved myself from going to Bainbridge prison, which was close by, and to which I should surely have been taken had it been known that I was making my escape.

Disguising His Race

Leaving Bainbridge, I proceeded about forty miles, travelling all day under a scorching sun through the woods, in which I saw many deer and serpents, until I reached Thomas Town in the evening. I there inquired the way to Augusta of a man whom I met, and also asked where I could obtain lodgings, and was told that there was a poor minister about a mile from the place who would give me lodgings. I accordingly went

and found them in a little log-house, where, having awakened
the family, I found them all lying on the bare boards, where I
joined them for the remainder of the night.

In the morning the old gentleman prayed for me that I
might be preserved on my journey; he had previously asked
me where I was going, and I knowing, that if I told him the
right place, any that inquired of him for me would be able
to find me, asked the way to Augusta instead of Savannah,
my real destination. I also told him that I was partly Indian
and partly white, but I am also partly African; but this I
omitted to tell him, knowing if I did I should be apprehended. After I had left this hut, I again inquired for Augusta, for the purpose of misleading my pursuers, but I afterwards took my course through the woods, and came into
a road, called the Coffee road, which General Jackson cut
down for his troops, at the time of the war between the
Americans and Spaniards, in Florida; in which road there
are but few houses, and which I preferred for the purpose of
avoiding detection.

After several days I left this road and took a more direct
way to Savannah, where I had to wade through two rivers
before I came to the Alatamah, which I crossed in a ferry-
boat about a mile below the place where the rivers Oconee
and Ocmulgee run together into one river called the
Alatamah. I here met with some cattle drovers who were
collecting cattle to drive to Savannah. On walking on before
them, I began to consider in what way I could obtain a passport for Savannah and determined on the following plan:

I called at a cottage, and after I had talked some time with
the wife who began to feel greatly for me in consequence of
my telling her a little of my history, (her husband being out
hunting), I pretended to show her my passport, feeling for it
everywhere about my coat and hat and not finding it, I went
back a little way pretending to look for it, but came back
saying I was very sorry, but I did not know where it was. At
last the man came home, carrying a deer upon his shoulders,
which he brought into the yard and began to dress it. The
wife then went out to tell him my situation, and after long

persuasion he said he could not write, but that if I could tell his son what was in my passport he should write me one; and knowing that I should not be able to pass Savannah without one, and having heard several free colored men read theirs, I thought I could tell the lad what to write. The lad sat down and wrote what I told him, nearly filling a large sheet of paper for the passport and another sheet with recommendations. These being completed, I was invited to partake of some of the fresh venison, which the woman of the house had prepared for dinner, and having done so, and feeling grateful for their kindness, I proceeded on my way. Going along I took my papers out of my pocket, and looking at them, although I could not read a word, I perceived that the boy's writing was very unlike other writing that I had seen, and was greatly blotted besides; consequently I was afraid that these documents would not answer my purpose, and began to consider what other plan I could pursue to obtain another pass.

An Opportune River Crossing

I had now to wade through another river to which I came, and which I had great difficulty in crossing in consequence of the water overflowing the banks of several rivers to the extent of upwards of twenty miles. In the midst of the water I passed one night upon a small island, and the next day I went through the remainder of the water. On many occasions I was obliged to walk upon my toes, and consequently found the advantage of being six feet two inches high, and at other times was obliged to swim. In the middle of this extremity I felt it would be imprudent for me to return; for if my master was in pursuit of me, my safest place from him was in the water, if I could keep my head above the surface. I was, however, dreadfully frightened, and most earnestly prayed that I might be kept from a watery grave, and resolved that if again I landed, I would spend my life in the service of God.

Having through mercy again started on my journey, I met with the drovers, and having, whilst in the water, taken the pass out of my hat, and so dipped it in the water as to spoil it, I showed it to the men, and asked them where I could get another. They told me, that in the neighbourhood there lived a rich cotton merchant, who would write me one. They took me to him, and gave their word that they saw the passport before it was wet, (for I had previously showed it to them), upon which the cotton planter wrote a free pass and a recommendation, to which the cow-drovers affixed their marks.

The recommendation was as follows:

"John Roper, a very interesting young lad, whom I have seen and travelled with for eighty or ninety miles on his road from Florida, is a free man, descended from Indian and white. I trust, he will be allowed to pass on without interruption, being convinced from what I have seen that he is free, and though dark, is not an African. I had seen his papers before they were wetted."

These cow-drovers, who procured me the passport and recommendation from the cotton planter, could not read; and they were intoxicated when they went with me to him. I am part African, as well as Indian and white, my father being a white man, Henry Roper, Esq., Caswell county, North Carolina, U.S., a very wealthy slave-holder who sold me when quite a child for the strong resemblance I bore to him. My mother is part Indian, part African; but I dared not disclose that, or I should have been taken up. I then had eleven miles to go to Savannah, one of the greatest slave-holding cities in America, and where they are always looking out for runaway slaves. When at this city, I had travelled about five hundred miles. (The distance between these two places is much less than five hundred miles; but I was obliged to travel round about, in order to avoid being caught.) It required great courage to pass through this place. I went through the main street with apparent confidence, though much alarmed; did not stop at any house in the city, but went down immediately to the dock and inquired for a berth as a steward to a vessel to New York. I had been in this capacity before on the Appalachicola River. The person whom I asked to procure me a berth was steward of one of the New

York packets; he knew Captain Deckay of the schooner *Fox* and got me a situation on board that vessel in five minutes after I had been at the docks. The schooner *Fox* was a very old vessel, twenty-seven years old, laden with lumber and cattle for New York; she was rotten and could not be insured. The sailors were afraid of her, but I ventured on board, and five minutes after, we dropped from the docks into the river. My spirits then began to revive, and I thought I should get to a free country directly. We cast anchor in the stream to keep the sailors on, as they were so dissatisfied with the vessel, and lay there four days; during which time I had to go into the city several times, which exposed me to great danger, as my master was after me, and I dreaded meeting with him in the city.

Fearing the *Fox* would not sail before I should be seized, I deserted her, and went on board a brig sailing to Providence, that was towed out by a steamboat, and got thirty miles from Savannah. During this time I endeavoured to persuade the steward to take me as an assistant and hoped to have accomplished my purpose; but the captain had observed me attentively and thought I was a slave; he therefore ordered me, when the steamboat was sent back, to go on board her to Savannah, as the fine for taking a slave from that city to any of the free states is five hundred dollars. I reluctantly went back to Savannah among slave-holders and slaves. My mind was in a sad state, and I was under strong temptation to throw myself into the river. I had deserted the schooner *Fox*, and knew that the captain might put me into prison till the vessel was ready to sail; if this had happened, and my master had come to the jail in search of me, I must have gone back to slavery. But when I reached the docks at Savannah, the first person I met was the captain of the *Fox*, looking for another steward in my place. He was a very kind man, belonging to the free states, and inquired if I would go back to his vessel. This usage was very different to what I expected, and I gladly accepted his offer. This captain did not know that I was a slave. In about two days we sailed from Savannah for New York.

A Daring Disguise

William and Ellen Craft

William and Ellen Craft, fugitive slaves and committed abolitionists, devised one of the most daring escapes from slavery
in Underground Railroad history. Indeed, their 1848 flight
was audacious for being strictly "above ground": light-
skinned Ellen, disguised as an ailing white gentleman, and
William, posing as a loyal servant, traveled openly by train,
steamboat, and ferry all the way from Georgia to Philadelphia, staying in hotels along the journey. Because Ellen could
not read or write, she wore bandages to explain her inability
to sign papers as well as her dependence on the "slave"
accompanying her. Once in the Northeast, the Crafts were
embraced by leading abolitionists such as William Wells
Brown and William Lloyd Garrison, and became active in the
antislavery movement until the 1850 Fugitive Slave Law
drove them, along with many other famous fugitives, to
England.

William and Ellen Craft's autobiography, *Running a Thousand Miles for Freedom*, was published in London in 1860.
The following selection, excerpted from the book, describes
the initial stages of the Crafts' bold plan and the care with
which they settled on their mode of disguise. It also relates
two of the close calls they had with detection before they
have even departed from Georgia, incidents that were the first
real tests of the effectiveness of their ingenious subterfuge.

My wife was torn from her mother's embrace in childhood, and taken to a distant part of the country. She
had seen so many other children separated from their par-

William and Ellen Craft, *Running a Thousand Miles for Freedom*. London: William
Tweedie, 1860.

ents in this cruel manner, that the mere thought of her ever becoming the mother of a child, to linger out a miserable existence under the wretched system of American slavery, appeared to fill her very soul with horror; and as she had taken what I felt to be an important view of her condition, I did not, at first, press the marriage but agreed to assist her in trying to devise some plan by which we might escape from our unhappy condition and then be married.

The Dangers of Escape

We thought of plan after plan, but they all seemed crowded with insurmountable difficulties. We knew it was unlawful for any public conveyance to take us as passengers, without our master's consent. We were also perfectly aware of the startling fact, that had we left without this consent the professional slave-hunters would have soon had their ferocious bloodhounds baying on our track, and in a short time we should have been dragged back to slavery, not to fill the more favourable situations which we had just left, but to be separated for life, and put to the very meanest and most laborious drudgery; or else have been tortured to death as examples, in order to strike terror into the hearts of others and thereby prevent them from even attempting to escape from their cruel taskmasters. It is a fact worthy of remark, that nothing seems to give the slaveholders so much pleasure as the catching and torturing of fugitives. They had much rather take the keen and poisonous lash, and with it cut their poor trembling victims to atoms, than allow one of them to escape to a free country and expose the infamous system from which he fled.

The greatest excitement prevails at a slave-hunt. The slaveholders and their hired ruffians appear to take more pleasure in this inhuman pursuit than English sportsmen do in chasing a fox or a stag. Therefore, knowing what we should have been compelled to suffer, if caught and taken back, we were more than anxious to hit upon a plan that would lead us safely to a land of liberty.

But, after puzzling our brains for years, we were reluctantly driven to the sad conclusion that it was almost impossible to escape from slavery in Georgia and travel 1,000 miles across the slave States. We therefore resolved to get the consent of our owners, be married, settle down in slavery, and endeavour to make ourselves as comfortable as possible under that system; but at the same time ever to keep our dim eyes steadily fixed upon the glimmering hope of liberty and earnestly pray God mercifully to assist us to escape from our unjust thraldom.

We were married, and prayed and toiled on till December, 1848, at which time (as I have stated) a plan suggested itself that proved quite successful, and in eight days after it was first thought of we were free from the horrible trammels of slavery and glorifying God who had brought us safely out of a land of bondage.

An Ingenious Disguise

Knowing that slaveholders have the privilege of taking their slaves to any part of the country they think proper, it occurred to me that, as my wife was nearly white, I might get her to disguise herself as an invalid gentleman and assume [pretend] to be my master, while I could attend as his slave, and that in this manner we might effect our escape. After I thought of the plan, I suggested it to my wife, but at first she shrank from the idea. She thought it was almost impossible for her to assume that disguise and travel a distance of 1,000 miles across the slave States. However, on the other hand, she also thought of her condition. She saw that the laws under which we lived did not recognize her to be a woman, but a mere chattel to be bought and sold or otherwise dealt with as her owner might see fit. Therefore the more she contemplated her helpless condition, the more anxious she was to escape from it. So she said, "I think it is almost too much for us to undertake; however, I feel that God is on our side, and with his assistance, notwithstanding all the difficulties, we shall be able to succeed. Therefore, if you will purchase the disguise, I will try to carry out the plan."

But after I concluded to purchase the disguise, I was

afraid to go to any one to ask him to sell me the articles. It is unlawful in Georgia for a white man to trade with slaves without the master's consent. But, notwithstanding this, many persons will sell a slave any article that he can get the money to buy. Not that they sympathize with the slave, but merely because his testimony is not admitted in court against a free white person.

Watching for an Opportunity

Therefore, with little difficulty I went to different parts of the town, at odd times, and purchased things piece by piece (except the trowsers which she found necessary to make), and took them home to the house where my wife resided. She being a ladies' maid, and a favourite slave in the family, was allowed a little room to herself; and amongst other pieces of furniture, which I had made in my overtime, was a chest of drawers; so when I took the articles home, she locked them up carefully in these drawers. No one about the premises knew that she had anything of the kind. So when we fancied we had everything ready the time was fixed for the flight. But we knew it would not do to start off without first getting our master's consent to be away for a few days. Had we left without this, they would soon have had us back into slavery, and probably we should never have got another fair opportunity of even attempting to escape.

Some of the best slaveholders will sometimes give their favourite slaves a few days' holiday at Christmas time; so, after no little amount of perseverance on my wife's part, she obtained a pass from her mistress, allowing her to be away for a few days. The cabinet-maker with whom I worked gave me a similar paper, but said that he needed my services very much, and wished me to return as soon as the time granted was up. I thanked him kindly; but somehow I have not been able to make it convenient to return yet; and, as the free air of good old England agrees so well with my wife and our dear little ones, as well as with myself, it is not at all likely we shall return at present to the "peculiar institution" of chains and stripes.

The Obstacle of Illiteracy

On reaching my wife's cottage she handed me her pass, and I showed mine, but at that time neither of us were able to read them. It is not only unlawful for slaves to be taught to read, but in some of the States there are heavy penalties attached, such as fines and imprisonment, which will be vigorously enforced upon any one who is humane enough to violate the so-called law. . . .

However, at first, we were highly delighted at the idea of having gained permission to be absent for a few days; but when the thought flashed across my wife's mind, that it was customary for travellers to register their names in the visitors' book at hotels, as well as in the clearance or Customhouse book at Charleston, South Carolina—it made our spirits droop within us.

So, while sitting in our little room upon the verge of despair, all at once my wife raised her head, and with a smile upon her face, which was a moment before bathed in tears, said, "I think I have it!" I asked what it was. She said, "I think I can make a poultice and bind up my right hand in a sling, and with propriety ask the officers to register my name for me." I thought that would do.

It then occurred to her that the smoothness of her face might betray her; so she decided to make another poultice, and put it in a white handkerchief to be worn under the chin, up the cheeks, and to tie over the head. This nearly hid the expression of the countenance, as well as the beardless chin.

The poultice is left off in the engraving, because the likeness could not have been taken well with it on.

My wife, knowing that she would be thrown a good deal into the company of gentlemen, fancied that she could get on better if she had something to go over the eyes; so I went to a shop and bought a pair of green spectacles. This was in the evening.

Ellen Becomes a "Gentleman"

We sat up all night discussing the plan and making preparations. Just before the time arrived, in the morning, for us to leave, I cut off my wife's hair square at the back of the head and got her to dress in the disguise and stand out on the floor. I found that she made a most respectable looking gentleman.

My wife had no ambition whatever to assume this disguise and would not have done so had it been possible to have obtained our liberty by more simple means; but we knew it was not customary in the South for ladies to travel with male servants; and therefore, notwithstanding my wife's fair complexion, it would have been a very difficult task for her to have come off as a free white lady, with me as her slave; in fact, her not being able to write would have made this quite impossible. We knew that no public conveyance would take us, or any other slave, as a passenger without our master's consent. This consent could never be obtained to pass into a free State. My wife's being muffled in the poultices, &c., furnished a plausible excuse for avoiding general conversation, of which most Yankee travellers are passionately fond.

The Harassment of Free Blacks

There are a large number of free negroes residing in the southern States; but in Georgia (and I believe in all the slave States), every coloured person's complexion is *primâ facie* evidence of his being a slave; and the lowest villain in the country, should he be a white man, has the legal power to arrest and question, in the most inquisitorial and insulting manner, any coloured person, male or female, that he may find at large, particularly at night and on Sundays, without a written pass signed by the master or some one in authority; or stamped free papers certifying that the person is the rightful owner of himself.

If the coloured person refuses to answer questions put to him, he may be beaten, and his defending himself against this attack makes him an outlaw, and if he be killed on the spot, the murderer will be exempted from all blame; but after the coloured person has answered the questions put to him, in a most humble and pointed manner, he may then be taken to prison; and should it turn out, after further examination, that he was caught where he had no permission or legal right to be, and that he has not given what they term a satisfactory account of himself, the master will have to pay a fine. On his refusing to do this, the poor slave may be legally and severely flogged by public officers. Should the prisoner prove to be a free man, he is most likely to be both whipped and fined.

The great majority of slaveholders hate this class of persons with a hatred that can only be equalled by the condemned spirits of the infernal regions. They have no mercy upon, nor sympathy for, any negro whom they cannot enslave. They say that God made the black man to be a slave for the white, and act as though they really believed that all free persons of colour are in open rebellion to a direct command from heaven,

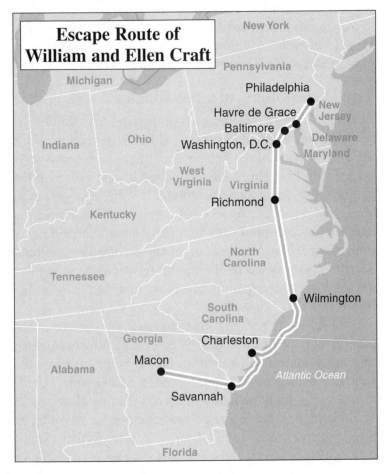

and that they (the whites) are God's chosen agents to pour out upon them unlimited vengeance. For instance, a Bill has been introduced in the Tennessee Legislature to prevent free negroes from travelling on the railroads in that State. It has passed the first reading. The bill provides that the President who shall permit a free negro to travel on any road within the jurisdiction of the State under his supervision shall pay a fine of 500 dollars, any conductor permitting a violation of the Act shall pay 250 dollars; provided such free negro is not under the control of a free white citizen of Tennessee, who will vouch for the character of said free negro in a penal bond of one thousand dollars. The State of Arkansas has passed a law to banish all free negroes from its bounds, and it came into effect on the 1st day of January, 1860. Every free negro found there after that date will be liable to be sold into slavery, the crime of freedom being unpardonable. The Missouri Senate has before it a bill providing that all free negroes above the age of eighteen years who shall be found in the State after September, 1860, shall be sold into slavery; and that all such negroes as shall enter the State after September, 1861, and remain there twenty-four hours, shall also be sold into slavery for ever. Mississippi, Kentucky, and Georgia, and in fact, I believe all the slave States, are legislating in the same manner. Thus the slaveholders make it almost impossible for free persons of colour to get out of the slave States in order that they may sell them into slavery if they don't go. If no white persons travelled upon railroads except those who could get some one to vouch for their character in a penal bond of one thousand dollars, the railroad companies would soon go to the "wall." Such mean legislation is too low for comment; therefore I leave the villainous acts to speak for themselves. . . .

Hopes and Fears

When the time had arrived for us to start, we blew out the lights, knelt down, and prayed to our Heavenly Father mercifully to assist us, as he did his people of old, to escape from cruel bondage; and we shall ever feel that God heard and answered our prayer. Had we not been sustained by a kind, and I sometimes think special, providence, we could never have overcome the mountainous difficulties which I am now about to describe.

After this we rose and stood for a few moments in breathless silence—we were afraid that some one might have been about the cottage listening and watching our movements. So I took my wife by the hand, stepped softly to the door, raised the latch, drew it open, and peeped out. Though there were trees all around the house, yet the foliage scarcely moved; in fact, everything appeared to be as still as death. I then whispered to my wife, "Come, my dear, let us make a desperate leap for liberty!" But poor thing, she shrank back, in a state of trepidation. I turned and asked what was the matter, she made no reply, but burst into violent sobs, and threw her head upon my breast. This appeared to touch my very heart; it caused me to enter into her feelings more fully than ever. We both saw the many mountainous difficulties that rose one after the other before our view and knew far too well what our sad fate would have been were we caught and forced back into our slavish den. Therefore on my wife's fully realizing the solemn fact that we had to take our lives, as it were, in our hands, and contest every inch of the thousand miles of slave territory over which we had to pass, it made her heart almost sink within her. . . .

However, the sobbing was soon over, and after a few moments of silent prayer she recovered her self-possession and said, "Come, William, it is getting late, so now let us venture upon our perilous journey."

We then opened the door and stepped as softly out as "moonlight upon the water." I locked the door with my own key, which I now have before me, and tiptoed across the yard into the street. I say tiptoed, because we were like persons near a tottering avalanche, afraid to move, or even breathe freely, for fear the sleeping tyrants should be aroused and come down upon us with double vengeance for daring to attempt to escape in the manner which we contemplated.

We shook hands, said farewell, and started in different directions for the railway station. I took the nearest possible way to the train for fear I should be recognized by some one, and got into the negro car in which I knew I should have to ride; but my *master* (as I will now call my wife) took a longer way round, and only arrived there with the bulk of the passengers. He obtained a ticket for himself and one for his slave to Savannah, the first port, which was about two hundred miles off. My master then had the luggage stowed away, and stepped into one of the best carriages.

But just before the train moved off I peeped through the window, and, to my great astonishment, I saw the cabinet-maker with whom I had worked so long, on the platform. He stepped up to the ticketseller and asked some question and then commenced looking rapidly through the passengers and into the carriages. Fully believing that we were caught, I shrank into a corner, turned my face from the door, and expected in a moment to be dragged out. The cabinet-maker looked into my master's carriage but did not know him in his new attire, and, as God would have it, before he reached mine the bell rang, and the train moved off.

I have heard since that the cabinet-maker had a presentiment that we were about to "make tracks for parts unknown," but, not seeing me, his suspicions vanished until he received the startling intelligence that we had arrived freely in a free State.

Another Close Call

As soon as the train had left the platform, my master looked round in the carriage and was terror-stricken to find a Mr. Cray—an old friend of my wife's master, who dined with the family the day before, and knew my wife from childhood—sitting on the same seat.

The doors of the American railway carriages are at the ends. The passengers walk up the aisle, and take seats on either side; and as my master was engaged in looking out of the window, he did not see who came in.

My master's first impression after seeing Mr. Cray was that he was there for the purpose of securing him. However, my master thought it was not wise to give any information respecting himself, and for fear that Mr. Cray might draw him into conversation and recognise his voice, my master resolved to feign deafness as the only means of self-defence.

After a little while, Mr. Cray said to my master, "It is a very fine morning, sir." The latter took no notice, but kept looking out of the window. Mr. Cray soon repeated this remark, in a little louder tone, but my master remained as before. This indifference attracted the attention of the passengers near, one of whom laughed out. This, I suppose, annoyed the old gentleman, so he said, "I will make him hear," and in a loud tone of voice repeated, "It is a very fine morning, sir."

My master turned his head, and with a polite bow said, "Yes," and commenced looking out of the window again.

One of the gentlemen remarked that it was a very great deprivation to be deaf. "Yes," replied Mr. Cray, "and I shall not trouble that fellow any more." This enabled my master to breathe a little easier and to feel that Mr. Cray was not his pursuer after all.

Learning About Abolitionists

The gentlemen then turned the conversation upon the three great topics of discussion in first-class circles in Georgia, namely, Niggers, Cotton, and the Abolitionists.

My master had often heard of abolitionists but in such a connection as to cause him to think that they were a fearful kind of wild animal. But he was highly delighted to learn from the gentlemen's conversation that the abolitionists were persons who were opposed to oppression, and, therefore, in his opinion, not the lowest, but the very highest, of God's creatures.

Without the slightest objection on my master's part, the gentlemen left the carriage at Gordon for Milledgeville (the capital of the State).

We arrived at Savannah early in the evening and got into an omnibus, which stopped at the hotel for the passengers to take tea. I stepped into the house and brought my master something on a tray to the omnibus, which took us in due time to the steamer, which was bound for Charleston, South Carolina.

Chapter 3

Peril and Punishment

Chapter Preface

Despite the hardships and indignities of enslavement, the decision to escape was seldom taken lightly. Factors to be weighed by the prospective runaway included not only certain physical punishment and likely resale to a distant owner under possibly even harsher conditions, but also emotional ties to family, fellow bondpersons, place, and occasionally, even to a master. Yet while it is not known how many runaways failed in attempts to flee, it is safe to say that most recognized that the probability of recapture was high, given the ubiquity of slave patrols, the unavailability of clear and direct routes, and the physical difficulties of the journey itself. Most runaways traveled by night and by foot, with little or no assistance from others as they made their way toward free states. Accounts by Underground Railroad operators such as Levi Coffin and Laura S. Haviland frequently describe fugitives arriving at safe houses with their clothes in tatters, their feet bare, and in sometimes desperate need of food and medical attention. Another great unknown figure of Underground Railroad history is how many runaway slaves died from starvation, illness, or physical injury sustained along the long journey. Many aspiring runaways in the Deep South chose Mexico and the Caribbean as their ultimate destinations because the daunting odds against successful escape were augmented even further by the distance between enslavement and the North.

What is striking, however, is that in several of the better-known slave narratives, such as those by Moses Roper and William Wells Brown, recapture and punishment were not sufficient to quell the determination to escape. Even more remarkably, the most famous conductor of all, Harriet Tubman, who was herself a fugitive, repeatedly risked her own freedom in order to venture back into slave territory to lead others out of captivity.

A Failed Escape

William Wells Brown

William Wells Brown was, after Frederick Douglass, the leading black American writer, orator, and abolitionist of his time. He lectured powerfully at antislavery meetings in the northeastern United States and abroad, where he had fled after the Fugitive Slave Law of 1850 made him subject to recapture. A prolific writer and exceptional literary stylist, Brown published drama, fiction, and travelogues in addition to his widely popular autobiography *Narrative of William W. Brown, a Fugitive Slave*, from which the following selection is excerpted.

Brown was born a slave in Lexington, Kentucky, to a black mother and white slaveholder. He spent most of his first two decades in St. Louis, where he had several masters, along with the opportunity to witness the horrors of the slave trade firsthand along the Mississippi to New Orleans. In the following selection, Brown describes the circumstances surrounding his first attempt at escape: his sister's imminent sale to an owner in distant Natchez that would wrench her from her family, and her urging that Brown take their mother and try to escape the fate of being sold farther south. Once Brown convinces his mother, he relates the secrecy and exhilaration of escape that was unfortunately cut short by recapture and despair. Shortly following their forced return to St. Louis, Brown's mother was sold as a field-worker and shipped to New Orleans, after which he never saw her again. But in 1834 he successfully escaped to the Great Lakes area of New York, where he worked on a Buffalo steamboat and more covertly, as a conductor on the Underground Railroad. By 1843 he was

William Wells Brown, *Narrative of William W. Brown, a Fugitive Slave*. London: Charles Gilpin, 1849.

an active abolitionist speaker; his 1847 autobiography, published both in America and Great Britain, won him internationally renown.

I was sent home, and was glad enough to leave the service of one who was tearing the husband from the wife, the child from the mother, and the sister from the brother—but a trial more severe and heart-rending than any which I had yet met with awaited me. My dear sister had been sold to a man who was going to Natchez and was lying in jail awaiting the hour of his departure. She had expressed her determination to die rather than go to the Far South, and she was put in jail for safe keeping. I went to the jail the same day that I arrived, but as the jailor was not in, I could not see her.

I went home to my master in the country, and the first day after my return, he came where I was at work and spoke to me very politely. I knew from his appearance that something was the matter. After talking about my several journeys to New Orleans with Mr. Walker, he told me that he was hard pressed for money, and as he had sold my mother and all her children except me, he thought it would be better to sell me than any other one, and that as I had been used to living in the city, he thought it probable that I would prefer it to a country life. I raised up my head and looked him full in the face. When my eyes caught his, he immediately looked to the ground. After a short pause, I said,

"Master, mother has often told me that you are a near relative of mine, and I have often heard you admit the fact; and after you have hired me out and received, as I once heard you say, nine hundred dollars for my services—after receiving this large sum, will you sell me to be carried to New Orleans or some other place?"

"No," said he, "I do not intend to sell you to a negro trader. If I had wished to have done that, I might have sold you to Mr. Walker for a large sum, but I would not sell you to a negro trader. You may go to the city and find you a good master."

"But," said I, "I cannot find a good master in the whole city of St. Louis."

"Why?" said he.

"Because there are no good masters in the State."

"Do you not call me a good master?"

"If you were, you would not sell me."

"Now I will give you one week to find a master in, and surely you can do it in that time."

The price set by my evangelical master upon my soul and body was the trifling sum of five hundred dollars. I tried to enter into some arrangement by which I might purchase my freedom, but he would enter into no such arrangement.

A Slave's Family Crisis

I set out for the city with the understanding that I was to return in a week with some one to become my new master. Soon after reaching the city, I went to the jail to learn if I could once more see my sister but could not gain admission. I then went to mother and learned from her that the owner of my sister intended to start for Natchez in a few days.

I went to the jail again the next day, and Mr. Simonds, the keeper, allowed me to see my sister for the last time. I cannot give a just description of the scene at that parting interview. Never, never can be erased from my heart the occurrences of that day! When I entered the room where she was, she was seated in one corner, alone. There were four other women in the same room, belonging to the same man. He had purchased them, he said, for his own use. She was seated with her face towards the door where I entered, yet she did not look up until I walked up to her. As soon as she observed me, she sprung up, threw her arms around my neck, leaned her head upon my breast, and, without uttering a word, burst into tears. As soon as she recovered herself sufficiently to speak, she advised me to take mother and try to get out of slavery. She said there was no hope for herself—that she must live and die a slave. After giving her some advice and taking from my finger a ring and placing it upon hers, I bade her farewell forever and returned to my mother, and then and there made up my mind to leave for Canada as soon as possible.

I had been in the city nearly two days, and as I was to be absent only a week, I thought best to get on my journey as soon as possible. In conversing with mother, I found her unwilling to make the attempt to reach a land of liberty, but she counselled me to get my liberty if I could. She said, as all her children were in slavery, she did not wish to leave them. I could not bear the idea of leaving her among those pirates when there was a prospect of being able to get away from them. After much persuasion, I succeeded in inducing her to make the attempt to get away.

In Search of Liberty

The time fixed for our departure was the next night. I had with me a little money that I had received, from time to time, from gentlemen for whom I had done errands. I took my scanty means and purchased some dried beef, crackers, and

A family of slaves waits to be sold at auction. Oftentimes families were torn apart when members were sold to different owners.

cheese, which I carried to mother who had provided herself with a bag to carry it in. I occasionally thought of my old master and of my mission to the city to find a new one. I waited with the most intense anxiety for the appointed time to leave the land of slavery in search of a land of liberty.

The time at length arrived, and we left the city just as the clock struck nine. We proceeded to the upper part of the city, where I had been two or three times during the day, and selected a skiff to carry us across the river. The boat was not mine, nor did I know to whom it did belong, neither did I care. The boat was fastened with a small pole, which, with the aid of a rail, I soon loosened from its moorings. After hunting round and finding a board to use as an oar, I turned to the city, and bidding it a long farewell, pushed off my boat. The current running very swift, we had not reached the middle of the stream before we were directly opposite the city.

Following the North Star

We were soon upon the Illinois shore, and, leaping from the boat, turned it adrift, and the last I saw of it, it was going down the river at good speed. We took the main road to Alton, and passed through just at daylight, when we made for the woods, where we remained during the day. Our reason for going into the woods was that we expected that Mr. Mansfield (the man who owned my mother) would start in pursuit of her as soon as he discovered that she was missing. He also knew that I had been in the city looking for a new master, and we thought probably he would go out to my master's to see if he could find my mother, and in so doing, Dr. Young might be led to suspect that I had gone to Canada to find a purchaser.

We remained in the woods during the day, and as soon as darkness overshadowed the earth, we started again on our gloomy way, having no guide but the North Star. We continued to travel by night, and secrete ourselves in woods by day; and every night, before emerging from our hiding-place, we would anxiously look for our friend and leader— the North Star. . . .

A Difficult Journey

As we travelled towards a land of liberty, my heart would at times leap for joy. At other times, being, as I was, almost constantly on my feet, I felt as though I could travel no further. But when I thought of slavery with its Democratic whips, its Republican chains, its evangelical blood-hounds, and its religious slave-holders—when I thought of all this paraphernalia of American Democracy and Religion behind me, and the prospect of liberty before me, I was encouraged to press forward, my heart was strengthened, and I forgot that I was tired or hungry.

On the eighth day of our journey, we had a very heavy rain, and in a few hours after it commenced, we had not a dry thread upon our bodies. This made our journey still more unpleasant. On the tenth day, we found ourselves entirely destitute of provisions, and how to obtain any we could not tell. We finally resolved to stop at some farmhouse and try to get something to eat. We had no sooner determined to do this, then we went to a house and asked them for some food. We were treated with great kindness, and they not only gave us something to eat but gave us provisions to carry with us. They advised us to travel by day and lie by at night. Finding ourselves about one hundred and fifty miles from St. Louis, we concluded that it would be safe to travel by daylight and did not leave the house until the next morning. We travelled on that day through a thickly settled country and through one small village. Though we were fleeing from a land of oppression, our hearts were still there. My dear sister and two beloved brothers were behind us, and the idea of giving them up and leaving them forever made us feel sad. But with all this depression of heart, the thought that I should one day be free and call my body my own buoyed me up and made my heart leap for joy. I had just been telling mother how I should try to get employment as soon as we reached Canada, and how I intended to purchase us a little farm, and how I would earn money enough to buy [my] sister and brothers, and how happy we would be in our own free home—when three men came up on horseback and ordered us to stop.

The Capture of the Runaways

I turned to the one who appeared to be the principal man and asked him what he wanted. He said he had a warrant to take us up. The three immediately dismounted, and one took from his pocket a handbill advertising us as runaways and offering a reward of two hundred dollars for our apprehension and delivery in the city of St. Louis. The advertisement had been put out by Isaac Mansfield and John Young.

While they were reading the advertisement, mother looked me in the face and burst into tears. A cold chill ran over me and such a sensation I never experienced before and I hope never to again. They took out a rope and tied me, and we were taken back about six miles to the house of the individual who appeared to be the leader. We reached there about seven o'clock in the evening, had supper, and were separated for the night. Two men remained in the room during the night. Before the family retired to rest, they were all called together to attend prayers. The man who but a few hours before had bound my hands together with a strong cord read a chapter from the Bible and then offered up prayer, just as though God sanctioned the act he had just committed upon a poor panting, fugitive slave.

The next morning, a blacksmith came in and put a pair of handcuffs on me, and we started on our journey back to the land of whips, chains, and Bibles. Mother was not tied but was closely watched at night. We were carried back in a wagon, and after four days travel, we came in sight of St. Louis. I cannot describe my feelings upon approaching the city.

As we were crossing the ferry, Mr. Wiggins, the owner of the ferry, came up to me and inquired what I had been doing that I was in chains. He had not heard that I had run away. In a few minutes, we were on the Missouri side and were taken directly to the jail. On the way thither, I saw several of my friends who gave me a nod of recognition as I passed them. After reaching the jail, we were locked up in different apartments.

Boston Protests the Return of Anthony Burns to Slavery

Charlotte Forten

On May 24, 1854, a runaway slave named Anthony Burns was arrested in Boston. Having escaped from Virginia about two months before, Burns was apprehended on his way home from his job in a Boston clothing store. Almost instantly Burns's arrest galvanized the city's many fervent abolitionists, including attorney Richard Henry Dunn, Baptist minister Leonard Grimes, and writers John Greenleaf Whittier and Henry David Thoreau. Angry activists both black and white took to the streets of Boston. A group of black protestors stormed the courthouse in attempt to free the captive Burns, and the ensuing confrontation with federal marshals resulted in thirteen arrests and one officer's death. Soon Boston was teeming with outraged abolitionists and armed soldiers under orders to keep the protestors at bay during Burns's trial the week following his arrest. Despite the widespread furor, federal judge Edward G. Loring ruled that under the 1850 Fugitive Slave Law, Burns had to be returned to his owner in Virginia.

Thousands of Bostonians turned out on June 2, 1854, to protest as Burns, under heavy military guard, was escorted toward a Virginia-bound ship. Black crepe and inverted American flags were displayed on buildings along the prisoner's route to the harbor. Church bells rang in mourning, and a large coffin on which the word "Liberty" had been written swayed over State Street. Although many of the protesters

Charlotte Forten, *The Journal of Charlotte Forten*, edited by Ray Allen Billington. New York: Dryden Press, 1953.

were committed abolitionists rallied by the antislavery Boston Vigilance Committee, the Burns case also affected countless citizens theretofore relatively apathetic toward the slavery controversy. The trial and return to slavery of Anthony Burns represented the infringement of Southern proslavery interests on the autonomy and popular will of the North. If in theory the Fugitive Slave Law was designed to pacify the South and demoralize not only slaves but the Northerners working tirelessly to assist runaways, in reality the Burns incident had proven the opposite. Significantly, Anthony Burns would be the last fugitive slave to be arrested in Massachusetts.

Protests continued even after Burns was sent back to Virginia. Frederick Douglass and William Lloyd Garrison published furious editorials in their respective antislavery newspapers. Leading abolitionist Wendell Phillips collected signatures on a petition that would eventually force Judge Loring's removal from the bench. By February 1855, Reverend Grimes had raised sufficient money to buy Burns's freedom.

The following selection of the uproar over the Burns incident comes from the journals of Charlotte Forten, who would become one of the most accomplished African American women of her time. The granddaughter of prominent black abolitionist and businessman James Forten, Charlotte was herself an antislavery activist as well as an educator who would be the first black teacher of white students in Salem, Massachusetts. At the time of the Burns incident, the seventeen-year-old Charlotte was living in Salem with abolitionist and Underground Railroad operator Charles Lenox Remond and his sister Sarah.

Thursday, May 25, 1854. Did not intend to write this evening, but have just heard of something which is worth recording—something which must ever rouse in the mind of every true friend of liberty and humanity, feelings of the deepest indignation and sorrow. Another fugitive from bondage has been arrested; a poor man, who for two short months has trod the soil and breathed the air of the "Old

Bay State," was arrested like a criminal in the streets of her capital, and is now kept strictly guarded—a double police force is required, the military are in readiness; and all this done to prevent a man, whom God has created in his own image, from regaining that freedom with which he, in common with every other human being, is endowed. I can only hope and pray most earnestly that Boston will not again disgrace herself by sending him back to a bondage worse than death; or rather that she will redeem herself from the disgrace which his arrest alone has brought upon her. . . .

Reaction to Burns's Arrest

Saturday, May 27. Returned home, read the Anti-Slavery papers, and then went down to the depot to meet father; he had arrived in Boston early in the morning, regretted very much that he had not reached there the evening before to attend the great meeting at Faneuil Hall. He says that the excitement in Boston is very great; the trial of the poor man takes place on Monday. We scarcely dare to think of what may be the result; there seems to be nothing too bad for these Northern tools of slavery to do. . . .

Tuesday, May 30. Rose very early and was busy until nine o'clock; then, at Mrs. Putnam's urgent request, went to keep store for her while she went to Boston to attend the Anti-Slavery Convention. I was very anxious to go, and will certainly do so tomorrow; the arrest of the alleged fugitive will give additional interest to the meetings, I should think. His trial is still going on and I can scarcely think of anything else; read again today as most suitable to my feelings and to the times, "The Run-away Slave at Pilgrim's Point," by [poet] Elizabeth B. Browning; how powerfully it is written! how earnestly and touchingly does the writer portray the bitter anguish of the poor fugitive as she thinks over all the wrongs and sufferings that she has endured, and of the sin to which tyrants have driven her but which they alone must answer for! It seems as if no one could read this poem without having his sympathies aroused to the utmost in behalf of the oppressed. After a long conversation with my friends on her return, on this all-absorbing subject, we separated for the night, and I went to bed, weary and sad.

Wednesday, May 31. Sarah and I went to Boston in the morning. Everything was much quieter—[more] outwardly than we expected, but still much real indignation and excitement prevail. We walked past the Court-House, which is now lawlessly converted into a prison, and filled with soldiers, some of whom were looking from the windows, with an air of insolent authority which made my blood boil, while I felt the strongest contempt for their cowardice and servility. We went to the meeting, but the best speakers were absent, engaged in the most arduous and untiring efforts in behalf of the poor fugitive; but though we missed the glowing eloquence of [abolitionist orators] Phillips, Garrison, and Parker, still there were excellent speeches made, and our hearts responded to the exalted sentiments of Truth and Liberty which were uttered. The exciting intelligence which occasionally came in relation to the trial, added fresh zeal to the speakers, of whom Stephen Foster and his wife were the principal. The latter addressed, in the most eloquent language, the women present, entreating them to urge their husbands and brothers to action, and also to give their aid on all occasions in our just and holy cause. I did not see father the whole day; he, of course, was deeply interested in the trial. Dined at Mr. Garrison's; his wife is one of the loveliest persons I have ever seen, worthy of such a husband. At the table, I watched earnestly the expression of that noble face, as he spoke beautifully in support of the nonresistant principles to which he has kept firm; his is indeed the very highest Christian spirit, to which I cannot hope to reach, however, for I believe in "resistance to tyrants," and would fight for liberty until death. We came home in the evening, and felt sick at heart as we passed through the streets of Boston on our way to the depot, seeing the military as they rode along, ready at any time to prove themselves the minions of the South.

Thursday, June 1st. The trial is over at last; the commissioner's decision will be given tomorrow. We are all in the greatest suspense; what will that decision be? Alas! that any one should have the power to decide the right of a fellow being to himself! It is thought by many that he will be acquitted of the *great crime* of leaving a life of bondage, as the legal evidence is not thought sufficient to convict him. But it is only too probable that they will sacrifice him to propitiate the South, since so many at the North dared oppose the passage of the infamous Nebraska Bill. . . .

Massachusetts Bows to Slave Interests

Friday, June 2. Our worst fears are realized; the decision was against poor Burns, and he has been sent back to a bondage worse, a thousand times worse than death. Even an attempt at rescue was utterly impossible; the prisoner was completely surrounded by soldiers with bayonets fixed, a cannon loaded, ready to be fired at the slightest sign. Today Massachusetts has again been disgraced. Again has she shewed her submission to the Slave Power; and Oh! with what deep sorrow do we think of what will doubtless be the fate of that poor man, when he is again consigned to the horrors of Slavery. With what scorn must that government be regarded, which cowardly assembles thousands of soldiers to satisfy the demands of slaveholders; to deprive of his freedom a man, created in God's own image, whose sole offense is the color of his skin! And if resistance is offered to this outrage, these soldiers are to shoot down American citizens without mercy; and this by the express orders of a government which proudly boasts of being the freest in the world; this on the very soil where the Revolution of 1776 began, in sight of the battle-field, where thousands of brave men fought and died in opposing British tyranny, which was nothing compared with the American oppression of today. In looking over my diary, I perceive that I did not mention that there was on the Friday night after the man's arrest, an attempt made to rescue him, but although it failed, on account of there not being men enough engaged in it, all honor should be given to those who bravely made attempt. I can write no more. A cloud seems hanging over me, over all our persecuted race, which nothing can dispel.

The Tragedy of Margaret Garner

Levi Coffin

Although Levi Coffin's *Reminiscences* (1876) contained many uplifting accounts of ingenious escapes and hard-won liberty, the famed Quaker Railroad conductor's description of the fate of Margaret Garner is a poignant reminder of the dangers and heartbreak that faced fugitive slaves even in free states such as Ohio. A group of slaves, including Garner, her husband, and their four children, had made an apparently successful journey from Kentucky to Ohio. But, as Coffin recounts, the slaves' owners, reinforced by a posse, tracked the runaways across the border. A despondent Margaret Garner fatally slashed the throat of her youngest child before her apprehenders intervened to prevent her from killing all the children and herself, as was her intent, rather than have them all forced back into slavery. Garner ended up succumbing to illness on the voyage back to her owner. Over a hundred years later, the tragic incident would inspire Pulitzer Prize–winning novelist Toni Morrison to pen *Beloved* based on the desperate act of Margaret Garner.

Perhaps no case that came under my notice, while engaged in aiding fugitive slaves, attracted more attention and aroused deeper interest and sympathy than the case of Margaret Garner, the slave mother who killed her child rather than see it taken back to slavery. This happened in the latter part of January, 1856. The Ohio River was frozen over at the time, and the opportunity thus offered for escaping to a free State was embraced by a number of slaves living in

Levi Coffin, *Reminiscences of Levi Coffin*. Cincinnati: Levi Coffin, 1876.

Kentucky, several miles back from the river. A party of seventeen, belonging to different masters in the same neighborhood, made arrangements to escape together. There was snow on the ground and the roads were smooth, so the plan of going to the river on a sled naturally suggested itself. The time fixed for their flight was Sabbath night, and having managed to get a large sled and two good horses, belonging to one of their masters, the party of seventeen crowded into the sled and started on their hazardous journey in the latter part of the night. They drove the horses at full speed, and at daylight reached the River below Covington, opposite Wester Row. They left the sled and horses here, and as quickly as possible crossed the river on foot. It was now broad daylight, and people were beginning to pass about the streets and the fugitives divided their company that they might not attract so much notice.

An old slave named Simon and his wife Mary, together with their son Robert and his wife Margaret Garner and four children, made their way to the house of a colored man named Kite, who had formerly lived in their neighborhood and had been purchased from slavery by his father, Joe Kite. They had to make several inquiries in order to find Kite's house, which was below Mill Creek, in the lower part of the city. This afterward led to their discovery; they had been seen by a number of persons on their way to Kite's, and were easily traced by pursuers. The other nine fugitives were more fortunate. They made their way up town and found friends who conducted them to safe hiding places, where they remained until night. They were put on the Underground Railroad, and went safely through to Canada. . . .

An Act of Desperation

In a few minutes . . . [Kite's] house was surrounded by pursuers—the masters of the fugitives, with officers and a posse of men. The door and windows were barred, and those inside refused to give admittance. The fugitives were determined to fight, and to die, rather than to be taken back to slavery. Margaret, the mother of the four children, declared that she would kill herself and her children before she would return to bondage. The slave men were armed and fought bravely. The window was first battered down with a stick of wood, and one of the deputy marshals attempted to enter, but a pistol shot from within made a flesh wound on his arm and caused him to abandon the attempt. The pursuers then battered down the door with some timber and rushed in. The husband of Margaret fired several shots, and wounded one of the officers, but was soon overpowered and dragged out of the house. At this moment, Margaret Garner, seeing that their hopes of freedom were in vain, seized a butcher knife that lay on the table, and with one stroke cut the throat of her little daughter, whom she probably loved the best. She then attempted to take the life of the other children and to kill herself, but she was overpowered and hampered before she could complete her desperate work. The whole party was then arrested and lodged in jail.

The trial lasted two weeks, drawing crowds to the courtroom every day. . . . The counsel for the defense brought witnesses to prove that the fugitives had been permitted to visit the city at various times previously. It was claimed that Margaret Garner had been brought here by her owners a number of years before, to act as nurse girl, and according to the law which liberated slaves who were brought into free States by the consent of their masters, she had been free from that time, and her children, all of whom had been born since then—following the condition of the mother—were likewise free.

The Commissioner decided that a voluntary return to slavery, after a visit to a free State, re-attached the conditions of slavery, and that the fugitives were legally slaves at the time of their escape. . . .

But in spite of touching appeals, of eloquent pleadings, the Commissioner remanded the fugitives back to slavery. He said that it was not a question of feeling to be decided by the chance current of his sympathies; the law of Kentucky and the United States made it a question of property.

Accused of Helping Runaway Slaves

William Still

Philadelphian William Still, the freeborn son of a former
slave, was a businessman, writer, and among the most prominent black conductors of the Underground Railroad. His 1872
book *Underground Railroad Records* was one of the few
post–Civil War histories to call attention to the significant
involvement of the runaways themselves in their escape rather
than stressing, as most works did, the efforts of white abolitionists in Railroad operations. After the Civil War, Still continued to lobby for equal rights and full citizenship for black
Americans.

The following selection from Still's *Underground Railroad
Records* recounts the experiences of Samuel Green Jr., a slave
helped by the Railroad and its most famed conductor Harriet
Tubman to successfully escape to Canada. Yet after Green's
father, Samuel Sr., a minister who had purchased his freedom,
returned to Maryland following a visit with his fugitive son in
Canada, he was arrested by local authorities and charged both
with assisting runaways and possessing seditious antislavery
materials, including a copy of Harriet Beecher Stowe's *Uncle
Tom's Cabin*. The old minister was sentenced to ten years in
prison for these offenses. Still's account provides an example
of yet another risk incurred by fugitive slaves—that their family members who remained behind in slave states would be
punished in their stead, whether bondsmen or, like Reverend
Green, legally free.

William Still, *Underground Railroad Records*. Philadelphia: W. Still, 1872.

S amuel Green Alias Wesley Kinnard, August 28th, 1854. The passenger answering to the above name left Indian Creek, Chester County, Maryland, where he had been held to service or labor, by Dr. James Muse. One week had elapsed from the time he set out until his arrival in Philadelphia. Although he had never enjoyed school privileges of any kind, yet he was not devoid of intelligence. He had profited by his daily experiences as a slave, and withal, had managed to learn to read and write a little, despite law and usage to the contrary. Sam was about twenty-five years of age and by trade, a blacksmith. Before running away, his general character for sobriety, industry, and religion, had evidently been considered good, but in coveting his freedom and running away to obtain it, he had sunk far below the utmost limit of forgiveness or mercy in the estimation of the slave-holders of Indian Creek.

During his intercourse with the Vigilance Committee, while rejoicing over his triumphant flight, he gave, with no appearance of excitement, but calmly, and in a common-sense-like manner, a brief description of his master, which was entered on the record book substantially as follows: "Dr. James Muse is thought by the servants to be the worst man in Maryland, inflicting whipping and all manner of cruelties upon the servants."

Help from Tubman and the Railroad

While Sam gave reasons for this sweeping charge, which left no room for doubt, on the part of the Committee, of his sincerity and good judgment, it was not deemed necessary to make a note of more of the doctor's character than seemed actually needed, in order to show why Sam had taken passage on the Underground Rail Road. For several years, Sam was hired out by the doctor at blacksmithing; in this situation, daily wearing the yoke of unrequited labor, through the kindness of Harriet Tubman (sometimes called "Moses"), the light of the Underground Rail Road and Canada suddenly illuminated his mind. It was new to him, but he was quite too intelligent and liberty-loving, not to heed the valuable information which this sister of humanity imparted. Thenceforth he was in love with Canada, and likewise a decided admirer of the U.R. Road. Harriet was herself, a shrewd and fearless agent, and well understood the entire route from that part of the country to Canada. The spring previous, she had paid a visit to the very neighborhood in which Sam lived, expressly to lead her own brothers out of "Egypt." She succeeded. To Sam this was cheering and glorious news, and he made up his mind, that before a great while, Indian Creek should have one less slave and that Canada should have one more citizen. Faithfully did he watch an opportunity to carry out his resolution. In due time a good Providence opened the way, and to Sam's satisfaction he reached Philadelphia, having encountered no peculiar difficulties. The Committee, perceiving that he was smart, active, and promising, encouraged his undertaking, and having given him friendly advice aided him in the usual manner. Letters of introduction were given him, and he was duly forwarded on his way. He had left his father, mother, and one sister behind. Samuel and Catharine were the names of his parents. Thus far, his escape would seem not to affect his parents, nor was it apparent that there was any other cause why the owner should revenge himself upon them.

A Father Punished for His Son's Escape

The father was an old local preacher in the Methodist Church—much esteemed as an inoffensive, industrious man; earning his bread by the sweat of his brow, and contriving to move along in the narrow road allotted colored people bond or free, without exciting a spirit of ill will in the pro-slavery power of his community. But the rancor awakened in the breast of slave-holders in consequence of the high-handed step the son had taken, brought the father under suspicion and hate. Under the circumstances, the eye of Slavery could do nothing more than watch for an occasion to pounce upon him. It was not long before the desired opportunity presented itself. Moved by parental affection, the old man concluded to pay a visit to his boy, to see how he was faring in a distant land, and among strangers. This resolution he quietly carried into effect. He found his son in Canada, doing well; industrious; a man of sobriety, and following his father's footsteps religiously. That the old man's heart was delighted with what his eyes saw and his ears heard in Canada, none can doubt. But in the simplicity of his imagination, he never dreamed that this visit was to be made the means of his destruction. During the best portion of his days he had faithfully worn the badge of Slavery, had afterwards purchased his freedom, and thus become a free man. He innocently conceived the idea that he was doing no harm in availing himself not only of his God-given rights, but of the rights that he had also purchased by the hard toil of his own hands. But the enemy was lurking in ambush for him—thirsting for his blood. To his utter consternation, not long after his return from his visit to his son "a party of gentlemen from the New Market district, went at night to Green's house and made search, whereupon was found a copy of *Uncle Tom's Cabin*, etc." This was enough, the hour had come, wherein to wreak vengeance upon poor Green.

The Case Against Green

The course pursued and the result, may be seen in the following statement taken from the Cambridge (Maryland), "Democrat," of April 29th, 1857, and communicated by the writer to the "Provincial Freeman."

Sam Green

The case of the State against Sam Green (free negro) indicted for having in his possession, papers, pamphlets, and pictorial representations, having a tendency to create discontent, etc., among the people of color in the State, was tried before the court on Friday last.

This case was of the utmost importance, and has created in the public mind a great deal of interest—it being the first case of the kind ever having occurred in our county.

It appeared, in evidence, that this Green has a son in Canada to whom Green made a visit last summer. Since his return to this county, suspicion has fastened upon him, as giving aid and assisting slaves who have since absconded and reached Canada, and several weeks ago, a party of gentlemen from New Market district, went at night, to Green's house and made search, whereupon was found a volume of *Uncle Tom's Cabin*, a map of Canada, several schedules of routes to the North, and a letter from his son in Canada, detailing the pleasant trip he had, the number of friends he met with on the way, with plenty to eat, drink, etc., and concludes with a request to his father, that he shall tell other slaves, naming them, to come on, which slaves, it is well known, did leave shortly afterwards, and have reached Canada. The case was argued with great ability, the counsel on both sides displaying a great deal of ingenuity, learning, and eloquence. The first indictment was for having in possession the letter, map, and route schedules.

Notwithstanding the mass of evidence given, to show the prisoner's guilt, in unlawfully having in his possession these documents, and that nine-tenths of the community in which he lived, believed that he had a hand in the running away of slaves, it was the opinion of the court, that the law under which he was indicted, was not applicable to the case, and that he must, accordingly, render a verdict of not guilty.

He was immediately arraigned upon another indictment, for having in possession *Uncle Tom's Cabin*, and tried; in this case the court has not yet rendered a verdict, but holds it under *curia* till after the Somerset county court. It is to be hoped, the court will find the evidence in this case sufficient to bring it within the scope of the law under which the prisoner is indicted (that of 1842, chap. 272), and that the prisoner may meet his due reward—be what it may.

That there is something required to be done by our Legislators, for the protection of slave property, is evident from the variety of constructions put upon the statute in this case, and we trust, that at the next meeting of the Legislature there will be such amendments, as to make the law on this subject, perfectly clear and comprehensible to the understanding of everyone.

In the language of the assistant counsel for the State, "Slavery must be protected or it may be abolished."

Judgment Is Passed

From the same sheet, of May 20th, the terrible doom of Samuel Green is announced in the following words:

In the case of the State against Sam Green, (free negro) who was tried at the April term of the Circuit Court of this county, for having in his possession abolition pamphlets, among which was *Uncle Tom's Cabin*, [and] has been found guilty by the court, and sentenced to the penitentiary for the term of ten years—until the 14th of May, 1867.

The son, a refugee in Canada, hearing the distressing news of his father's sad fate at the hands of the relentless "gentlemen," often wrote to know if there was any prospect of his deliverance.

In this dark hour the friends of the Slave could do but little more than sympathize with this heart-stricken son and grey-haired father. The aged follower of the Rejected and Crucified had like Him to bear the "reproach of many," and make his bed with the wicked in the Penitentiary. Doubtless there were a few friends in his neighborhood who sympathized with him, but they were powerless to aid the old man. But thanks to a kind Providence, the great deliverance brought about during the Rebellion by which so many captives were freed, also unlocked Samuel Green's prison-doors and he was allowed to go free.

After his liberation from the Penitentiary, we had from his own lips narrations of his years of suffering—of the bitter cup, that he was compelled to drink, and of his being sustained by the almighty Arm—but no notes were taken at that time, consequently we have nothing more to add concerning him, save a faithful likeness.

An Angry Crowd Rescues a Captive Fugitive Slave

Sarah H. Bradford

Of all the names associated with the Underground Railroad, perhaps none is better known than Harriet Tubman, the fearless "conductor" who led over three hundred runaways to freedom. Born a slave in Dorchester County, Maryland, she was christened Araminta Ross, and worked both as a field hand and house servant. In her early teens she suffered a serious head injury when a two-pound weight that an overseer intended for another slave struck the slight Tubman instead. She recovered, but was prone her entire life to seizures that would produce brief comas. At around the age of fourteen, she married a free black man named John Tubman, but when she made her escape five years later, she was alone, on foot, guided by the North Star, and helped along her way to Pennsylvania by a benevolent white woman. In Philadelphia, Harriet Tubman (she had taken her mother's name by this time) found work as a servant, but a year after her own escape she stole back to Maryland to assist her sister and her sister's two children to freedom. Her career as a "conductor" had begun. Next she escorted her brother and another runaway to safety. Her husband, however, had remarried and declined to join her, but Tubman's mission no longer applied solely to her own kin. Soon she became known as the Moses of her people, as clever about eluding detection as she was dedicated to

Sarah H. Bradford, *Harriet, the Moses of Her People*. New York: G.R. Lockwood & Son, 1886.

helping slaves escape bondage. At one point a $40,000 reward was offered in the South for her apprehension, but neither she nor any of the runways she escorted was ever captured.

Although the majority of Northerners were not abolitionist even on the eve of the Civil War, the enactment of the Fugitive Slave Law found more and more ordinary people appalled to witness in their own home states the terrible spectacles of runways dragged back to slavery by bounty hunters. The following selection, from abolitionist schoolteacher Sarah H. Bradford's biography of Tubman, describes a remarkable, spontaneous demonstration of civil disobedience in 1860, as citizens of Troy, New York, joined with Tubman to prevent the return of fugitive slave Charles Nalle to the South. With Tubman at the helm, a crowd faced down United States Marshals in outright defiance of the Fugitive Slave Law's requirement that citizens assist in the apprehension of runaways. Amid the chaos Tubman's cool head helped to ensure Nalle's safe escape, but the open involvement of throngs of ordinary New Yorkers in thwarting the bounty hunters exemplifies an extraordinarily public, collective operation of the Underground Railroad.

In the spring of 1860, Harriet Tubman was requested by Mr. Gerrit Smith to go to Boston to attend a large Anti-Slavery meeting. On her way, she stopped at Troy to visit a cousin, and while there the colored people were one day startled with the intelligence that a fugitive slave, by the name of Charles Nalle, had been followed by his master (who was his younger brother, and not one grain whiter than he), and that he was already in the hands of the officers, and was to be taken back to the South. The instant Harriet heard the news, she started for the office of the United States Commissioner, scattering the tidings as she went. An excited crowd was gathered about the office, through which Harriet forced her way, and rushed up stairs to the door of the room where the fugitive was detained. A wagon was already waiting before the door to carry off the man, but the crowd was even then so great, and in such a state of excitement, that the officers did not dare to bring the man down. On the opposite side of the street stood the colored people, watching the window where they could see Harriet's sun-bonnet, and feeling assured that so long as she stood there, the fugitive was

---

Advertisements for Runaways

In addition to federal marshals, bounty hunters, and blood-hounds, fugitive slaves were also beset by countless, widely circulated advertisements for their capture, most offering rewards. The rewards underscored the cash "value" of slaves to the southern planter, and the descriptions of the runaways often reveal the kind of treatment they received, citing scars, brandings, and fetters as identifying marks. The following advertisement was placed by James Norcom, the sexually abusive owner of Harriet Jacobs.

$100 REWARD

Will be given for the apprehension and delivery of my Servant Girl HARRIET. She is a light mulatto, 21 years of age, about 5 feet 4 inches high, of a thick and corpulent habit, having on her head a thick covering of black hair that curls naturally, but which can be easily combed straight. She speaks easily and fluently, and has an agreeable carriage and address. Being a good seamstress, she has been accustomed to dress well, has a variety of very fine clothes, made in the prevailing fashion, and will probably appear, if abroad, tricked out in gay and fashionable finery. As this girl absconded from the plantation of my son without any known cause or provocation, it is probable she designs to transport herself to the North.

The above reward, with all reasonable charges, will be given for apprehending her, or securing her in any prison or jail within the U. States.

All persons are hereby forewarned against harboring or entertaining her, or being in any way instrumental in her escape, under the most rigorous penalties of the law.

American Beacon, July 4, 1835. Courtesy of the North Carolina Division of Archives and History.

still in the office. Time passed on, and he did not appear. "They've taken him out another way, depend upon that," said some of the colored people. "No," replied others, "there stands Moses yet, and as long as she is there, he is safe."

Tubman Intervenes

Harriet, now seeing the necessity for a tremendous effort for his rescue, sent out some little boys to cry fire. The bells rang, the crowd increased, till the whole street was a dense mass of people. Again and again the officers came out to try and clear the stairs, and make a way to take their captive down; others were driven down, but Harriet stood her ground, her head bent and her arms folded. "Come, old woman, you must get out of this," said one of the officers; "I must have the way cleared; if you can't get down alone, some one will help you." Harriet, still putting on a greater appearance of decrepitude, twitched away from him, and kept her place. Offers were made to buy Charles from his master, who at first agreed to take twelve hundred dollars for him; but when this was subscribed, he immediately raised the price to fifteen hundred. The crowd grew more excited. A gentleman raised a window and called out, "Two hundred dollars for his rescue, but not one cent to his master!" This was responded to by a roar of satisfaction from the crowd below.

The Fugitive Appears

At length the officers appeared, and announced to the crowd, that if they would open a lane to the wagon, they would promise to bring the man down the front way. The lane was opened, and the man was brought out—a tall, handsome, intelligent white man [i.e., fair-skinned black], with his wrists manacled together, walking between the U.S. Marshal and another officer, and behind him his brother and his master, so like him that one could hardly be told from the other. The moment they appeared, Harriet roused from her stooping posture, threw up a window, and cried to her friends: "Here he comes—take him!" and then darted down the stairs like a wild-cat. She seized one officer and pulled him down, then another, and tore him away from the man; and keeping her arms about the slave, she cried to her friends: "Drag us out! Drag him to the river! Drown him! but don't let them have him!" They were knocked down together, and while down, she tore off her sun-bonnet and tied it on the head of the fugitive. When he rose, only his head could be seen, and amid the surging mass of people the slave was no longer recognized, while the master appeared like the slave. Again and again they were knocked down, the poor slave utterly helpless, with his manacled wrists, streaming with blood. Harriet's outer clothes were torn from her, and even her stout shoes were pulled from her feet, yet she never relinquished her hold of the man, till she had dragged him to the river, where he was tumbled into a boat, Harriet following in a ferry-boat to the other side. But the telegraph was ahead of them, and as soon as they landed he was seized and hurried from her sight.

A Frantic Rescue

After a time, some school children came hurrying along, and to her anxious inquiries they answered, "He is up in that house, in the third story." Harriet rushed up to the place. Some men were attempting to make their way up the stairs. The officers were firing down, and two men were lying on the stairs, who had been shot. Over their bodies our heroine rushed, and with the help of others burst open the door of the room, and dragged out the fugitive, whom Harriet carried down stairs in her arms. A gentleman who was riding by with a fine horse, stopped to ask what the disturbance meant; and on hearing the story, his sympathies seemed to be thoroughly aroused; he sprang from his wagon, calling out, "That is a blood-horse, drive him till be drops." The poor man was hurried in; some of his friends jumped in after him, and drove at the most rapid rate to Schenectady.

Chapter 4

Conductors and Friends

Chapter Preface

In the past, scholarship on the Underground Railroad not only tended to focus on the conductors rather than the fugitives, but also overemphasized the contributions of white abolitionists, especially Quakers, in the Railroad's operations. Yet the abolitionist movement as a whole was not representative of the majority of Northern white views toward slavery, particularly prior to the enactment of the Fugitive Slave Act of 1850. Even on the brink of the Civil War many Northerners regarded abolitionists as troublemakers and radicals whose meddling in the Southern institution of slavery only worsened the nation's sectional tensions. Among the reasons President Abraham Lincoln initially resisted declaring that slavery, not secession, was the cause of the war was that he feared most Northerners would refuse to support a conflict being waged over emancipation. Even when the Emancipation Proclamation was issued in 1862, it was extremely unpopular throughout the North (as was Lincoln himself for his management of the war effort), lending momentum to the 1864 challenge for the presidency by former Union general George B. McClellan, who opposed emancipation.

Among the many conundrums for Underground Railroad scholarship has been attempting to establish precise numbers and identities of those who assisted runaways. (Most historians agree that around three thousand individuals likely served as Railroad conductors.) A handful of names are well known: Harriet Tubman, William Still, William Wells Brown, Levi Coffin, Thomas Garrett, Quaker feminist Lucretia Mott, writer Henry David Thoreau, and Allan Pinkerton, founder of the famous detective agency. Yet many of the names of those who provided aid to fugitive slaves remain unknown, another consequence of the clandestine nature of Railroad operations.

A Friend of the Slaves

Levi Coffin

As far back as colonial times, the Quakers were passionate
opponents of slavery; it is no accident that so many white
abolitionists in antebellum America belonged to the Society
of Friends. Levi Coffin was born in slaveholding North Carolina, but the Quaker schoolteacher found the institution
repugnant. While still in North Carolina, he struggled to open
a school for slaves, but he was thwarted by owners who
denied their chattel permission to attend. Moving with his
wife to Newport, Indiana, in 1826, Coffin found himself situated along the most frequently traveled escape route for runaways trying to get to Canada. Soon the Coffins' home
became a major "station" along the Underground Railroad. It
has been estimated that Levi Coffin gave safe harbor to over
three thousand runaway slaves, providing them with shelter,
food, and clothing to sustain them along their northward journey. In the following selection from his *Reminiscences*
(1876), Coffin vividly describes the fugitives' travails, the
route they generally followed, the "signals" of their arrival,
and the risks both for the runways and those who abetted
them. His anecdote about the timorous fellow Quaker who
supported him in principle but not necessarily in practice is
suggestive, exemplifying not only the moral duty abolitionists
felt to come to the aid of fugitive slaves, but also the reticence
many otherwise decent, upstanding white Northerners felt
about violating laws that they acknowledged as unjust.

Levi Coffin, *Reminiscences of Levi Coffin*. Cincinnati: Levi Coffin, 1876.

In the winter of 1826–27, fugitives began to come to our house, and as it became more widely known on different routes that the slaves fleeing from bondage would find a welcome and shelter at our house, and be forwarded safely on their journey, the number increased. Friends in the neighborhood, who had formerly stood aloof from the work, fearful of the penalty of the law, were encouraged to engage in it when they saw the fearless manner in which I acted, and the success that attended my efforts. They would contribute to clothe the fugitives and would aid in forwarding them on their way but were timid about sheltering them under their roof; so that part of the work devolved on us. Some seemed really glad to see the work go on, if somebody else would do it. Others doubted the propriety of it and tried to discourage me and dissuade me from running such risks. They manifested great concern for my safety and pecuniary interests, telling me that such a course of action would injure my business and perhaps ruin me; that I ought to consider the welfare of my family; and warning me that my life was in danger, as there were many threats made against me by the slave-hunters and those who sympathized with them.

The Duties of a Good Samaritan

After listening quietly to these counselors, I told them that I felt no condemnation for anything that I had ever done for the fugitive slaves. If by doing my duty and endeavoring to fulfill the injunctions of the Bible, I injured my business, then let my business go. As to my safety, my life was in the hands of my Divine Master, and I felt that I had his approval. I had no fear of the danger that seemed to threaten my life or my business. If I was faithful to duty, and honest and industrious, I felt that I would be preserved and that I could make enough to support my family. At one time there came to see me a good old Friend who was apparently very deeply concerned for my welfare. He said he was as much opposed to slavery as I was but thought it very wrong to harbor fugitive slaves. No one there knew of what crimes they were guilty; they might have killed their masters or committed some other atrocious deed, then those who sheltered them and aided them in their escape from justice would indirectly be accomplices. He mentioned other objections which he wished me to consider and then talked for some time, trying to convince me of the errors of my ways. I heard him patiently until he had relieved his mind of the burden upon it and then asked if he thought the Good Samaritan stopped to inquire whether the man who fell among thieves was guilty of any crime before he attempted to help him? I asked him if he were to see a stranger who had fallen into the ditch would he not help him out until satisfied that he had committed no atrocious deed? These and many other questions which I put to him, he did not seem able to answer satisfactorily. He was so perplexed and confused that I really pitied the good old man, and advised him to go home and read his Bible thoroughly, and pray over it, and I thought his concern about my aiding fugitive slaves would be removed from his mind and that he would feel like helping me in the work. We parted in good feeling, and he always manifested warm friendship toward me until the end of his days.

Operating the Underground Railroad

Many of my pro-slavery customers left me for a time, my sales were diminished, and for a while my business prospects were discouraging, yet my faith was not shaken nor my efforts for the slaves lessened. New customers soon came in to fill the places of those who had left me. New settlements were rapidly forming to the north of us, and our own was filling up with emigrants from North Carolina and other States. My trade increased, and I enlarged my business. I was blessed in all my efforts and succeeded beyond my expectations. The Underground Railroad business increased as time advanced, and it was attended with heavy expenses, which I could not have borne had not my affairs been prosperous. I found it necessary to keep a team and a wagon always at command to convey the fugitive slaves on their journey. Sometimes, when we had large companies, one or two other teams and wagons were required. These journeys had to be made at night, often through deep mud and bad roads and along by-ways that were seldom traveled. Every precaution to evade pursuit had to be used, as the hunters were often on the track and sometimes ahead of the slaves. We had different routes for sending the fugitives to depots, ten, fifteen, or twenty miles distant, and when we heard of slave-hunters having passed on one road, we forwarded our passengers by another.

In some instances where we learned that the pursuers were ahead of them, we sent a messenger and had the fugitives brought back to my house to remain in concealment until the bloodhounds in human shape had lost the trail and given up the pursuit.

Harboring the Runaways

I soon became extensively known to the friends of the slaves, at different points on the Ohio River where fugitives generally crossed, and to those northward of us on the various routes leading to Canada. Depots were established on the different lines of the Underground Railroad, south and north of Newport, and a perfect understanding was maintained between those who kept them. Three principal lines from the South converged at my house; one from Cincinnati, one from Madison, and one from Jeffersonville, Indiana. The roads were always in running order, the connections were good, the conductors active and zealous, and there was no lack of passengers. Seldom a week passed without our receiving passengers by this mysterious road. We found it necessary to be always prepared to receive such company and properly care for them. We knew not what night or what hour of the night we would be roused from slumber by a gentle rap at the door. That was the signal announcing the arrival of a train of the Underground Railroad, for the locomotive did not whistle nor make any unnecessary noise. I have often been awakened by this signal and sprang out of bed in the dark and opened the door. Outside in the cold or rain, there would be a two-horse wagon loaded with fugitives, perhaps the greater part of them women and children. I would invite them, in a low tone, to come in, and they would follow me into the darkened house without a word, for we knew not who might be watching and listening. When they were all safely inside and the door fastened, I would cover the windows, strike a light and build a good fire. By this time my wife would be up and preparing victuals for them, and in a short time the cold and hungry fugitives would be made comfortable. I would accompany the conductor of the train to the stable and care for the horses that had, perhaps, been driven twenty-five or thirty miles that night, through the cold and rain. The fugitives would rest on pallets before the fire the rest of the night. Frequently, wagon-loads of passengers from the different lines have met at our house, having no previous knowledge of each other. The companies varied in number, from two or three fugitives to seventeen.

Travelers in Rags

The care of so many necessitated much work and anxiety on our part, but we assumed the burden of our own will and bore it cheerfully. It was never too cold or stormy or the hour of night too late for my wife to rise from sleep and provide food and comfortable lodging for the fugitives. Her sympathy for those in distress never tired, and her efforts in their behalf never abated. This work was kept up during the time we lived at Newport, a period of more than twenty years. The number of fugitives varied considerably in different years, but the annual average was more than one hundred. They generally came to us destitute of clothing and were often barefooted. Clothing must be collected and kept on hand, if possible, and money must be raised to buy shoes and purchase goods to make garments for women and children. The young ladies in the neighborhood organized a sewing society and met at our house frequently to make clothes for the fugitives.

Sometimes when the fugitives came to us destitute, we kept them several days until they could be provided with comfortable clothes. This depended on the circumstances of danger. If they had come a long distance and had been out several weeks or months—as was sometimes the case—and it was not probable that hunters were on their track, we thought it safe for them to remain with us until fitted for traveling through the thinly settled country to the North. Sometimes fugitives have come to our house in rags, foot-sore and toil-worn, and almost wild, having been out for several months traveling at night, hiding in canebrakes or thickets during the day, often being lost and making little headway at night, particularly in cloudy weather, when the North Star could not be seen, sometimes almost perishing for want of food, and afraid of every white person they saw, even after they came into a free State, knowing that slaves were often captured and taken back after crossing the Ohio River.

A Mother's Determination

Such as these we have kept until they were recruited in strength, provided with clothes, and able to travel. When they first came to us they were generally unwilling to tell their stories or let us know what part of the South they came from. They would not give their names or the names of their masters, correctly, fearing that they would be betrayed. In several instances fugitives came to our house sick from exhaustion and exposure and lay several weeks. One case was that of a woman and her two children—little girls. Hearing that her children were to be sold away from her, she determined to take them with her and attempt to reach Canada. She had heard that Canada was a place where all were free, and that by traveling toward the North Star, she could reach it. She managed to get over the Ohio River with her two little girls and then commenced her long and toilsome journey northward. Fearing to travel on the road, even at night, lest she should meet somebody, she made her way through the woods and across fields, living on fruits and green corn, when she could procure them, and sometimes suffering severely for lack of food. Thus she wandered on and at last reached our neighborhood. Seeing a cabin where some colored people lived she made her way to it. The people received her kindly and at once conducted her to our house. She was so exhausted by the hardships of her long journey, and so weak-

Letter to William Still

Although the Underground Railroad was an informal network, precise if often coded communications between operators were imperative to assisting fugitives and evading would-be captors. William Still of Philadelphia and Joseph C. Bustill of Harrisburg were two leading black conductors in Pennsylvania. Bustill's letter to Still, reproduced below, conveys precise information about the shepherding of a small group of runaways North. The careful timing to which Bustill refers is a reminder of the urgency of keeping the fugitives moving ahead of those pursuing them well into Northern territory.

Harrisburg, Pennsylvania
March 24, 1856

Friend Still:
    I suppose ere this you have seen those five large and three small packages I sent by way of Reading, consisting of three men and women and children. They arrived here this morning at 8½ o'clock and left twenty minutes past three. You will please send me any information likely to prove interesting in relation to them.

Lately we have formed a Society here, called the Fugitive Aid Society. This is our first case, and I hope it will prove entirely successful.

When you write, please inform me what signs or symbols you make use of in your dispatches, and any other information in relation to operations of the Underground Rail Road.

Our reason for sending by the Reading Road, was to gain time; it is expected the owners will be in town this afternoon, and by this Road we gained five hours' time, which is a matter of much importance, and we may have occasion to use it sometimes in the future. In great haste, Yours with great respect,

JOS. C. BUSTILL

William Still, *The Underground Railroad*. Philadelphia, 1872.

ened by hunger, having denied herself to feed her children, that she soon became quite sick. Her children were very tired but soon recovered their strength and were in good health. . . .

Other Friends of the Railroad

The fugitives generally arrived in the night, and were secreted among the friendly colored people or hidden in the upper room of our house. They came alone or in companies and in a few instances had a white guide to direct them.

One company of twenty-eight that crossed the Ohio River at Lawrenceburg, Indiana—twenty miles below Cincinnati—had for conductor a white man whom they had employed to assist them. The company of twenty-eight slaves referred to, all lived in the same neighborhood in Kentucky and had been planning for some time how they could make their escape from slavery. This white man—John Fairfield—had been in the neighborhood for some weeks buying poultry, etc., for market, and though among the whites he assumed to be very pro-slavery, the negroes soon found that he was their friend.

He was engaged by the slaves to help them across the Ohio River, and conduct them to Cincinnati. They paid him some money which they had managed to accumulate. The amount was small, considering the risk the conductor assumed, but it was all they had. Several of the men had their wives with them, and one woman a little child with her, a few months old. John Fairfield conducted the party to the Ohio River, opposite the mouth of the Big Miami, where he knew there were several skiffs tied to the bank near a woodyard. The entire party crowded into three large skiffs or yawls and made their way slowly across the river. The boats were overloaded and sank so deep that the passage was made in much peril. The boat John Fairfield was in was leaky and began to sink when a few rods from the Ohio bank, and he sprang out on the sand-bar where the water was two or three feet deep, and tried to drag the boat to the shore. He sank to his waist in mud and quick-sands and had to be pulled out by some of the negroes. The entire party waded out through mud and water and reached the shore safely, though all were wet and several lost their shoes. They hastened along the bank toward Cincinnati, but it was now late in the night and daylight appeared before they reached the city.

Their plight was a most pitiable one. They were cold, hungry, and exhausted; those who had lost their shoes in the mud suffered from bruised and lacerated feet while, to add to their discomfort, a drizzling rain fell during the latter part of the night. They could not enter the city, for their appearance would at once proclaim them to be fugitives. When they reached the outskirts of the city, below Mill Creek, John Fairfield hid them as well as he could in ravines that had been washed in the sides of the steep hills and told them not to move until he returned. He then went directly to John Hatfield, a worthy colored man, a deacon in the Zion Baptist church, and told his story. He had applied to Hatfield before and knew him to be a great friend to the fugitives—one who had often sheltered them under his roof and aided them in every way he could. When he arrived, wet and muddy, at John Hatfield's house, he was scarcely recognized. He soon made himself and his errand known, and Hatfield at once sent a messenger to me, requesting me to come to his house without delay, as there were fugitives in danger. I went at once and met several prominent colored men who had also been summoned. While dry clothes and a warm breakfast were furnished to John Fairfield, we anxiously discussed the situation of the twenty-eight fugitives who were lying hungry and shivering in the hills in sight of the city.

A Community Rallies to Help

Several plans were suggested, but none seemed practicable. At last I suggested that some one should go immediately to a certain German livery stable in the city and hire two coaches, and that several colored men should go out in buggies and take the women and children from their hiding-places, then that the coaches and buggies should form a procession as if going to a funeral and march solemnly along the road leading to Cumminsville, on the west side of the

Mill Creek. In the western part of Cumminsville was the Methodist Episcopal burying-ground where a certain lot of ground had been set apart for the use of the colored people. They should pass this and continue on the Colerain Pike till they reached a right-hand road leading to College Hill. At the latter place they would find a few colored families, living in the outskirts of the village, and could take refuge among them. Jonathan Cable, a Presbyterian minister, who lived near Farmer's College, on the west side of the village, was a prominent Abolitionist, and I knew that he would give prompt assistance to the fugitives.

I advised that one of the buggies should leave the procession at Cumminsville, after passing the burying ground, and hasten to College Hill to apprise friend Cable of the coming of the fugitives, that he might make arrangements for their reception in suitable places. My suggestions and advice were agreed to and acted upon as quickly as possible.

While the carriages and buggies were being procured, John Hatfield's wife and daughter, and other colored women of the neighborhood, busied themselves in preparing provisions to be sent to the fugitives. A large stone jug was filled with hot coffee, and this, together with a supply of bread and other provisions, was placed in a buggy and sent on ahead of the carriages, that the hungry fugitives might receive some nourishment before starting. The conductor of the party, accompanied by John Hatfield, went in the buggy, in order to apprise the fugitives of the arrangements that had been made and have them in readiness to approach the road as soon as the carriages arrived. Several blankets were provided to wrap around the women and children whom we knew must be chilled by their exposure to the rain and cold. The fugitives were very glad to get the supply of food; the hot coffee especially was a great treat to them, and much revived them. About the time they finished their breakfast, the carriages and buggies drove up. . . .

All the arrangements were carried out, and the party reached College Hill in safety and were kindly received and cared for.

The Route to Freedom

When it was known by some of the prominent ladies of the village that a large company of fugitives were in the neighborhood, they met together to prepare some clothing for them. Jonathan Cable ascertained the number and size of the shoes needed, and the clothes required to fit the fugitives for traveling, and came down in his carriage to my house, knowing that the Anti-Slavery Sewing Society had their depository there. I went with him to purchase the shoes that were needed and my wife selected all the clothing we had that was suitable for the occasion; the rest was furnished by the noble women of College Hill.

I requested friend Cable to keep the fugitives as secluded as possible until a way could be provided for safely forwarding them on their way to Canada. Friend Cable was a stockholder in the Underground Railroad, and we consulted together about the best route, finally deciding on the line by way of Hamilton, West Elkton, Eaton, Paris, and Newport, Indiana. I wrote to one of my particular friends at West Elkton, informing him that I had some valuable stock on hand which I wished to forward to Newport, and requested him to send three two-horse wagons—covered—to College Hill, where the stock was resting, in charge of Jonathan Cable.

The three wagons arrived promptly at the time mentioned and a little after dark took in the party, together with another fugitive who had arrived the night before, and whom we added to the company. They went through to West Elkton safely that night, and the next night reached Newport, Indiana. With little delay they were forwarded on from station to station through Indiana and Michigan to Detroit, having fresh teams and conductors each night and resting during the day. I had letters from different stations, as they progressed, giving accounts of the arrival and departure of the train, and I also heard of their safe arrival on the Canada shore.

The Underground Railroad in the Midwest

Laura S. Haviland

The Midwestern United States were of vital importance to the
Underground Railroad. The upper Midwestern states shared a
border with Canada, the ultimate destination for many thousands of fugitive slaves. Because Windsor, Ontario, was just
across the river from Detroit, the Underground Railroad in
Michigan was especially active. Canadian-born Laura S. Haviland and her husband Charles established Michigan's first
Underground Railroad "station" in 1834. A devout Quaker,
Haviland also was a teacher who taught black as well as
white children at the Raisin Institute, which she founded in
1837, and later at schools in Ohio. Her dedication to abolitionism and service to the Underground Railroad prompted
Southern slaveholders to put up a $3,000 reward for her
capture.

In the following selection, which is an excerpt from her
memoir, Haviland describes the informal but painstaking
organization and coordination of a group of Quaker conductors in the Midwest, who included Levi and Catherine Coffin.
With the Ohio River a main crossing point from slaveholding
Kentucky, more Underground Railroad stations operated in
Ohio than in any other state. Also noteworthy in the passage
are the elaborate ruses undertaken by the fugitives along with
the conductors in order to elude the patrollers and disarm
their owners. George (whom his owner calls "Tom") returns

Laura S. Haviland, *A Woman's Life-Work: Labors and Experiences of Laura S. Haviland.*
Cincinnati: Walden & Stove, 1884.

to his master under the guise of preferring slavery to the false promises of abolitionists, a pretense that enables him to assist his wife Liz (from whom he claims to be estranged) to freedom. From Haviland's remembrances emerges a picture of an intricate system of signs, signals, disguise, and collaboration carefully designed to throw off the "biped bloodhounds," as Haviland terms the bounty hunters.

As my married children had charge of the farm, and the younger ones were in school, and well provided for, I spent a few months in mission work and nursing the sick. My dear friends, Levi and Catherine Coffin, had given me a very cordial invitation to make their house my home whenever I was in Cincinnati. Soon after my arrival, at early dawn, nine slaves crossed the river and were conducted to one of our friends on Walnut Hills for safety until arrangements could be made to forward them to Victoria's domain [Canada]. I called on them to see what was needed for their Northern march and found them filled with fear lest they should be overtaken. As there was a prospect before them of being taken down the river, they concluded to "paddle their own canoe." They had with them their five little folks that seemed as full of fear as were their trembling parents. A little girl of five years raised the window-shade to look out. When her mother discovered her she exclaimed, in a half-smothered voice, "Why, Em! you'll have us all kotched, if you don't mind;" and the little thing dropped behind a chair like a frightened young partridge hiding under a leaf at the mother's alarm of danger. While making our plans, we were greatly relieved to find that the well-known Quaker conductor, William Beard, was in the city, with a load of produce from his farm. This covered market-wagon was a safe car, that had borne many hundreds to his own depot, and was now ready for more valuable freight before the city should be filled with slave-hunters. But few weeks elapsed before we learned of the safe arrival of these two families that we fitted for their journey to Canada.

One of our vigilance committee came early one morning to inform us that there were two young men just arrived, who were secreted in the basement of Zion Baptist Church (colored). As their home was only twenty-five miles from the river, it was necessary to make all possible speed in removing them before Kentucky slave-hunters should block our track. I took their measures to procure for each a Summer suit, and went to our store of new and second-hand clothing, at Levi Coffin's, where anti-slavery women met tri-monthly to spend a day in making and repairing clothing for fugitive slaves. In early evening I took a large market-basket, with a suit for each, and had them conducted to a safer hiding-place until a way opened for them to go to a Friend's settlement about eighty miles distant, where George chose to remain and work a few months. But James would not risk his liberty by tarrying and censured George for running such a risk. "You needn't think your new name's gwine to save you when ole massa comes."

George's Secret

But little did James understand the deep-hidden reason that kept his friend George behind. He worked faithfully nearly a year, kept the suit I gave him for his Sunday suit, and used his old Kentucky suit for his work, patching them himself until patch upon patch nearly covered the old brown jeans of his plantation wear. When warm weather again returned, without revealing his design of going back to his master in Kentucky, for he knew his abolition friends would discourage his project, he took the eighty dollars he had earned since he left his master and wore the suit of clothes he brought away, and in the darkness of night went to his wife's cabin. Here he gave a full history of the kind friends who had paid good wages for his work and said he was going to take all to his master and tell him he was sick of freedom; "and you mus' be mighty mad," he went on, "'case I come back; and say, "If he's a mind to make sich a fool of his self, as to be so jubus, 'case I talked leetle while wid Jake, long time ago, as to run off an' leave me, he may go. He needn't think I'll take 'im back; I won't have nothin' to say to 'im, never!' An' I'll quarrel 'bout you too; an' when all ov 'em is done fussin' 'bout me comin' back, I'll steal to you in a dark night, an' lay a plan to meet on Lickin' River; an' we'll take a skiff an' muffle oars till we get to the Ohio; an' I knows jus' whar to go in any dark night, an' we'll be free together. I didn't tell Jim I's gwine to make massa b'leve all my lies to get you; for I tell you, Liz, I ain't got whole freedom without you."

Before eight o'clock A.M. George stood before his master, with his old name and old plantation suit, presenting him with the eighty dollars he had earned for his master since he had left his home, that he never wanted to leave again. For he had found "abolitioners the greates' rascals I ever seen. I wants no more ov' em. They tried hard to git me to Canada; but I got all I wants of Canada. An' I tell you, Massa Carpenter, all I wants is one good stiddy home. I don't want this money; it's yourn."

His master was well pleased, and told all his neighbors how happy his Tom [i.e., George's slave name] was to get back again, and gave all the money he had earned since he had been gone. It was a long time before neighboring planters had the confidence on Tom that his master had, and they told him that Tom should never step his foot on their plantations; but he told them all that he had perfect confidence in Tom's honesty.

'He came back perfectly disgusted with abolitionists; he said they will work a fellow half to death for low wages. And he even patched his old suit, himself, that he wore off. And I have found the reason why he left. He and Liz had a quarrel, and now he don't care a fig about her; and I heard yesterday that her master says he'll shoot him if he dares to come on his plantation. But he needn't worry; for you couldn't hire Tom to go near Liz."

Regaining His Master's Trust

Tom's master told him all the planters were afraid of him, and said he would play a trick on him yet.

"I'll stay at home, and won't even go out to meetin's, till

Runaway slaves escape to the North using the Underground Railroad, a system of safe houses and "conductors" who brought the slaves to the next stop.

all ov 'em will see I means I says."

"That's right, Tom; they don't know you like I do. But I told them 't would do all the niggers good just to hear your story about the meanness of abolitionists. You know, Tom, that was just what I told you, that they pretended to be your friends, but they were your worst enemies."

"Yes, massa, I al'us bleved you; and if Liz hadn't cut up the way she did I never'd tried 'em."

All things went on smoothly with Tom. He was never more trusty, diligent, and faithful in all that pertained to his master's interest. Three months still found him contented and happy, and the constant praise he received from his master to his neighbors began to inspire them with sufficient confidence to permit him to attend their meetings occasionally, though he did not appear anxious to enjoy that privilege until his master proposed his going, and then he was careful to attend only day meetings. Neighboring white people often talked with him about his Northern trip, and all got the story he had told his master, until Tom became quite a pet missionary, as his reports went far and near, among both whites and blacks. After Lizzie's master became quite satisfied with her hatred toward Tom, he allowed the hound, which he kept over two months to watch for Tom, to go back to the keeper. Though Tom and Lizzie lived eight miles apart, they had a secret dispatch-bearer, by whom they reported to each other; but visits were very few and far between. . . .

An Opportunity Arises

A few months after this there was a holiday, and Tom was so faithful, his master gave him permission to visit his aunt, six miles distant in an opposite direction from Lizzie's home, and she too got permission to visit her friends five miles away, but not toward's Tom's master. The plan laid in his midnight visit was to start after sundown, and go until dark in the direction of the place each had their permission to go, and then go for Licking River; and she was to go up the river, while he was to go down, until they met. He was to secure the first skiff with oars he could find to aid them down the river with all possible speed to the Ohio. They succeeded in making good time after they met, until day dawn overtook them, when they hid the skiff under a clump of bushes, and the oars they took the precaution to hide some distance away in case the skiff was discovered and taken away. They secreted themselves still further in the woods, but not so far but they could watch their tiny craft through the thicket. Much to their discomfiture a number of boys [found] their skiff and had a long hunt for the oars but, not succeeding, furnished themselves with poles and pushed out of sight to the great relief of the temporary owners, so near being discovered during the hunt for the oars. At ten o'clock, when all was still, they crept out of their hiding-place, took their oars, and hunted two hours before they found another skiff. Though smaller and harder to manage than the one they lost, yet they reached the Ohio just at sunrise. Two men on the opposite side of Licking River hallooed, "Where are you going?"

"To market, sir."

What have you got?"

"Butter an' eggs, sir."

As he saw them in the skiff and pushing toward them, he expected every moment to be overhauled, but he pulled with all his might for the opposite shore, and did not dare look back until they had reached the middle of the river, when, to their great relief, the two men had given up the chase and turned back and had almost reached the place of their starting. He said Lizzie trembled so hard that the coat over her shook, so great was her fear. Said Lizzie, "I reckon the owner of the coat shook as hard as I did when you was pullin' for life. I specs you sent fear clare down into them paddles you's sweattin' over;" and they had a good laugh over fright and success.

Temporary Safety

With George there was no fear after entering the basement of Zion Baptist Church, his old hiding-place. . . . A voice from the adjoining room was heard to say, "Come right in, Mrs. Haviland, we are not afraid of you;" and as the fugitive clasped my hand in both of his, I exclaimed, "Where have you seen me?"

"Don't you mind Jim and George you giv' a basket full of close to las' Summer? You giv' me the linen pants an' blue checked gingham coat and straw hat; an' you giv' Jim thin pants and coat and palm-leaf hat; and don't you mind we went out in a market-wagon to a Quaker settlement?"

"Yes, but how came you here again?"

"It was for this little woman I went back." Then he went over his managing process, as above related.

As I was soon to go to my home in Michigan, it was proposed by our vigilance committee that this couple, with Sarah, who made her escape over a year previously, should go with me. Sarah was to be sold away from her little boy of three years for a fancy girl, as she was beautiful octoroon and attractive in person. She knew full well the fate that awaited her and succeeded in escaping. She was an excellent house servant and highly respected by all who made her acquaintance for her sterling Christian character and general intelligence. She had lived in a quiet Christian family who gave her good wages, but she did not dare to risk her liberty within one hundred miles of her former home.

The Group of Refugees Grows

A few days after the arrival of George and wife, a mulatto woman and her daughter of sixteen, bound South from Virginia, left a steamer and joined our company. While waiting for a certan canal-boat, the owner and captain being friendly to our work, another young man joined us. These we received at different points to avoid suspicion. Before we reached the third bridge we were overtaken by Levi Coffin with another young man, whom he had instructed implicitly to regard all the lessons I might give him. I gave them all a charge to say nothing of going farther than Toledo, Ohio, and talk of no farther back than Cincinnati.

While on our way George pointed at a wire and told his wife it was a telegraph-wire, at which she dodged back and for a moment seemed as badly frightened as though her master had been in sight. It was a lucky thing for us that no stranger happened to be in sight, as her fright would have betrayed them. Even an assurance from George that the wires could do no harm could hardly satisfy her, until he appealed to me to confirm his statement that it was the operators at each end of the wires that gave information.

The day before we reached Toledo one of the drivers left, and the steersman employed our boy William with the consent of the captain. I told George to tell William I wanted to see him at the expiration of the time set for him to drive. He came into the cabin while the other passengers were on deck and told me all the hands seemed very clever, and the steersman told him he would find a good place for him to work in Toledo, and that he would see that he had good wages. He asked him various questions that led him to disclose his starting point, Vicksburg, Mississippi. As he was so very friendly, he answered all his queries, even to his master's name. This I had charged him not to give. As George and the other colored man saw the steersman and another man employed on the boat so very intimate, and careful to keep William with them, they began to fear for their own safety. There came up a sudden shower during William's time to drive, and he got thoroughly drenched; and as he had no change of garments, the steersman and the other boys of the boat furnished him out of their own wardrobe. It had now become difficult for me to secure an interview with William, on account of his close friends, and I became as fearful of the telegraph wires as was Mary, over whom we had a little sport.

But William began to fear all was not right, and regretted having told this man of his condition, and made an errand on deck, as he saw me sitting alone. He told me all he had said to the steersman. I told him to appear very careless and say nothing, but to appear as if he was going with the steersman as he had suggested. As we should be in Toledo in three hours, I would go into the city, and the women and George would follow me to a place of safety. Then I would return for my shawl, that I should leave on the boat. By that time, the passengers would all have left, and he and the other young man must remain about the boat. Then I would watch the opportunity, and when I went out, I should turn short corners but give them time to keep me in sight. Accordingly, I returned for my shawl but made no haste to leave until those close friends entered a saloon; then was our time; I gave them the wink and left for a place of safety.

A Glimpse of Freedom

After I had put one and two in a place, my next work was to solicit money to pay our fare to Canada, on a boat that was to leave at 9 A.M. the next day. Here were six fares to pay to Detroit, as Sarah had sufficient to pay her own. The friends in Cincinnati had paid their fare to Toledo. It was now nearly night, and I had but little time; but I succeeded by nine o'clock the next morning, leaving a colored man to conduct them to the boat; with hardly five minutes to spare I reached the boat with my living freight.

Once out in the lake we felt quite secure. Yet there was a

possibility of a telegram being sent to William's master and danger of being overtaken by officers in Detroit. Knowing of their anxiety to see Canada, I waited until we were near enough to see carriages and persons on the road on the other side. When I said to George's wife "There is Canada." "It ain't, is it?" "It is, certainly. It is where no slave-owner can claim his slave." She ran to her husband to tell the good news. But neither he nor the balance of them believed her, and all came running to me: "That ain't Canada, is it?" Being assured that the land of freedom was in full view, with tears of joy they gazed upon their "House of Refuge," and within forty minutes we were there. And to see them leap for joy was rich pay for all my care in their behalf. George and Jake had both armed themselves with deadly weapons, in case of an attempt to capture them, resolving on liberty or death. I left each with fifty cents and returned to my own sweet home.

Hardships at Home

I found the large building unfinished. As the first buildings were temporary, they were unsuitable for students to occupy another Winter, which would be the eleventh Winter our school had been in successful operation. Brother Patchin, our principal, was called to another field as pastor and teacher and would go if the new building was not ready for use by the following academic year. While these probabilities were under consideration, brother J.F. Dolbeare was taken from us after a short illness. As he was an important trustee and an active Christian worker, his loss was severely felt. We had a few months previously met with a similar loss in the death of another trustee, our valued friend and brother, Elijah Brownell, a minister of the Society of Friends. Surely dark clouds again overhung our favorite institution in which many of our students were taught in the school of Christ before they came to us, and many out of the hundreds who had enjoyed the privileges of our school, we had good reasons for believing, yielded their young hearts to the loving Savior's invitation while with us. With the undying interests of the youth so near my heart, it was a trial to have our school suspended a year; but what could I do? I must keep up the ten per cent interest on three hundred dollars of my indebtedness, and could not contract five hundred dollars more to finish the institution building erected on the acre of ground I had given for that object. It was inclosed, and a portion of the floors laid, and doors and windows cased. This had cost over one thousand dollars for a building thirty by fifty-six feet.

At the farm was still carried on by my married children, I conclude to return to Cincinnati and engaged in nursing the sick during the cold season, as the cough to which I was subject was returning. All things considered, the conclusion was reached to suspend Raisin Institute one year at least. An Oberlin scholarship was presented me for my daughter Laura Jane, who decided to take a gentlemen's collegiate course. Not only my financial pressure seemed to direct toward that more Southern field, but the cause of those who were thirsting for liberty and were almost daily leaving boats or crossing the river, was also a strong incentive to occupy a post near the Southern end of the road whose Northern terminus was in Queen Victoria's dominions.

A Wanted Woman

Many of my friends thought me presuming to venture so near those who had threatened my life repeated, and in the handbills of the Tennesseans (report said) there was offered $3,000 reward for my head. Thomas K. Chester stated in a letter that he had sent them to a number of the Southern States, to let them know what sort of sisters they had in the North. But J.F. Dolbeare, on the night before his death, called me to his bedside, and, taking my hand in his, said, "Sister Haviland, you have passed through close and trying places in your work, and your anti-slavery mission is not yet finished. Your trials are not over. Greater dangers are for you to pass through—I see it. O, may the Lord prepare you for the work he has for to accomplish! He has sustained you thus far. He will grant you his protecting arm. I know it." I have often had occasion to remember the words I listened to in that solemn hour, during thirty years that have since passed.

Making the Case for Freedom

Thomas Garrett

Along with Ohio's Levi Coffin, Thomas Garrett of Delaware remains among the most famous of the Quaker abolitionists and Underground Railroad operators. A Wilmington iron merchant, Garrett is believed to have assisted over two thousand fugitive slaves throughout the four decades preceding the Civil War. In neighboring Maryland, which, like Delaware, was a slave state, a $10,000 reward was posted for Garrett's capture. In 1848 the U.S. Circuit Court charged Garrett with the crime of assisting runaways. He was found guilty and ordered to pay a hefty fine of $5,400 that forced him to declare bankruptcy. Yet Garrett refused to recant his life's work, proclaiming before the presiding judge, "I say to thee, and to all in this court room, that if anyone knows a fugitive who wants shelter . . . send him to Thomas Garrett and he will befriend him." Garrett's many friends in the abolitionist community helped him salvage his ruined fortunes.

In the following selection, Garrett writes one of his friends, author Harriet Beecher Stowe, of an 1846 incident in which he and another Delaware antislavery activist, John Hunn, ran afoul of the local authorities for harboring a black family. Unlike the 1848 trial (in which Hunn too was charged and convicted), the abolitionists' attempts to secure freedom for their black friends ultimately persuaded the local judge to rule in favor of liberty.

Harriet Beecher Stowe, *The Key to Uncle Tom's Cabin*. Cleveland: Jewitt, Proctor, and Worthington, 1853.

Wilmington, Delaware,
1st month, 18th, 1853

M y Dear Friend, Harriet Beecher Stowe:
I have this day received a request from [Massachusetts abolitionist and reformer] Charles K. Whipple of Boston, to furnish thee with a statement, authentic and circumstantial, of the trouble and losses which have been brought upon myself and others of my friends from the aid we had rendered to fugitive slaves, in order, if thought of sufficient importance, to be published in a work thee is now preparing for the press. . . .

I will now endeavor to give thee a statement of what John Hunn and myself suffered by aiding a family of slaves a few years since. I will give the facts as they occurred and thee may condense and publish so much as thee may think useful in thy work, and no more:

A Family Seeks Help

In the 12th month, year 1846, a family, consisting of Samuel Hawkins, a freeman, his wife Emeline, and six children, who were afterwards *proved slaves*, stopped at the house of a friend named John Hunn, near Middletown, in this state, in the evening about sunset to procure food and lodging for the night. They were seen by some of Hunn's proslavery neighbors, who soon came with a constable, and had them taken before a magistrate. Hunn had left the slaves in his kitchen when he went to the village of Middletown, half a mile distant. When the officer came with a warrant for them, he met Hunn at the kitchen door, and asked for the blacks; Hunn, with truth, said he did not know where they were. Hunn's wife, thinking they would be safer, had sent them up stairs during his absence, where they were found. Hunn made no resistance, and they were taken before the magistrate, and from his office direct to Newcastle jail, where they arrived about one o'clock on 7th day morning.

The sheriff and his daughter, being kind, humane people, inquired of Hawkins and wife the facts of their case; and his daughter wrote to a lady here to request me to go to Newcastle and inquire into the case, as her father and self really believed they were most of them, if not all, entitled to their *freedom.* Next morning I went to Newcastle: had the family of colored people brought into the parlor, and the sheriff and myself came to the conclusion that the parents and four youngest children were by law entitled to their freedom. I prevailed on the sheriff to show me the commitment of the magistrate, which I found was defective, and not in due form according to law. I procured a copy and handed it to a lawyer. He pronounced the commitment irregular, and agreed to go next morning to Newcastle and have the whole family taken before Judge Booth, Chief Justice of the state, by habeas corpus, when the following admission was made by Samuel Hawkins and wife: They admitted that the two eldest boys were held by one Charles Glaudin, of Queen Anne County, Maryland, as slaves; that after the birth of these two children, Elizabeth Turner, also of Queen Anne, the mistress of their mother, had set her free, and permitted her to go and live with her husband, near twenty miles from her residence, after which the four youngest children were born; and that her mistress during all that time, eleven or twelve years, had never contributed one dollar to their support, or come to see them. After examining the commitment in their case, and consulting with my attorney, the judge set the whole family at liberty. The day was wet and cold; one of the children, three years old, was a cripple from white swelling [a chronic inflammation, usually of the knee], and could not walk a step; another, eleven months old, at the breast; and the parents being desirous of getting to Wilmington, five miles distant, I asked the judge if there would be any risk of impropriety in my hiring a conveyance for the mother and four young children to Wilmington. His reply, in the presence of the sheriff and my attorney, was there would not be any. I then requested the sheriff to procure a hack to take them over to Wilmington.

The Trial of a Quaker Hero

Harriet Beecher Stowe

The Connecticut-born daughter of noted minister Lyman Beecher, Harriet Beecher Stowe is best known as author of *Uncle Tom's Cabin*, the 1852 antislavery novel that galvanized the abolitionist movement and outraged slavery's defenders. Stowe was also a schoolteacher and friend to many prominent abolitionists.

Because many Southerners attacked the widely popular novel's harsh depiction of slavery as unrealistic, in 1853 Stowe responded to her critics with a nonfiction follow-up called *The Key to Uncle Tom's Cabin* that documented the cruelties of slavery on which she had based her novel. *The Key* also testifies to the dedication and self-sacrifice of many Quaker abolitionists who risked their livelihoods and liberty in order to assist runaway slaves. The following excerpt from *The Key* details such an example. A pious young Quaker man, Richard Dillingham, is charged, tried, and consequently convicted and sent to prison for his attempt to transport fugitive slaves to freedom. Drawing on letters written by Dilllingham and his family as well as a local newspaper report, Stowe employs many of the same devices that also made *Uncle Tom's Cabin* so popular and influential a novel such as open appeals to family, sentiment, and Christian piety.

Richard Dillingham was the son of a respectable Quaker family in Morrow County, Ohio. His pious mother brought him up in the full belief of the doctrine of St. John,

Harriet Beecher Stowe, *The Key to Uncle Tom's Cabin*. Cleveland: Jewitt, Proctor, and Worthington, 1853.

that the love of God and the love of man are inseparable. He was diligently taught in such theological notions as are implied in such passages as these:

> Hereby perceive we the love of God, because he laid down his life for us; and we ought also to lay down our lives for the brethren.— But whoso hath this world's goods and seeth his brother have need, and shutteth up his bowels of compassion from him, how dwelleth the love of God in him?—My little children, let us not love in word and in tongue, but in deed and in truth.

In accordance with these precepts, Richard Dillingham, in early manhood, was found in Cincinnati teaching the coloured people, and visiting in the prisons, and doing what in him lay to "love in deed and in truth."

Some unfortunate families among the coloured people had dear friends who were slaves in Nashville, Tennessee. Richard was so interested in their story, that when he went into Tennessee he was actually taken up and caught in the very fact of helping certain poor people to escape to their friends.

Dillingham Is Imprisoned

He was seized and thrown into prison. In the language of this world he was imprisoned as a "negro-stealer." His own account is given in the following letter to his parents:

Nashville Jail, 12th mo: 15th, 1849.

Dear Parents,

I presume you have heard of my arrest and imprisonment in the Nashville jail, under a charge of aiding in an attempted escape of slaves from the city of Nashville, on the 5th inst. I was arrested by M.D. Maddox (district constable), aided by Frederick Marshal, watchman at the Nashville Inn, and the bridge-keeper, at the bridge across the Cumberland river. When they arrested me, I had rode up to the bridge on horseback and paid the toll for myself and for the hack to pass over, in which three coloured persons, who were said to be slaves, were found by the men who arrested me. The driver of the hack (who is a free coloured man of this city), and the persons in the hack, were also arrested; and after being taken to the Nashville Inn and searched, we were all taken to jail. My arrest took place about eleven o'clock at night.

In another letter he says:

At the bridge, Maddox said to me, "You are just the man we wanted. We will make an example of you." As soon as we were safe in the bar-room of the Inn, Maddox took a candle and looked me in the face, to see if he could recognise my countenance; and looking intently at me a few moments, he said, "Well, you are too good-looking a young man to be engaged in such an affair as this." The by-standers asked me several questions, to which I replied that, under the present circumstances, I would rather be excused from answering any questions relating to my case; upon which they desisted from further inquiry. Some threats and malicious wishes were uttered against me by the ruffian part of the assembly, being about twenty-five persons. I was put in a cell which had six persons in it, and I can assure thee that they were very far from being agreeable companions to me, although they were kind. But thou knows that I do not relish cursing and swearing, and, worst of all, loathsome and obscene blasphemy and of such was most of the conversation of my prison mates when I was first put in here. The jailors are kind enough to me, but the jail is so constructed that it cannot be warmed, and we have either to warm ourselves by walking in our cell, which is twelve by fifteen feet, or by lying in bed. I went out on my trial on the 16th of last month, and put it off till the next term of the court, which will be commenced on the second of next 4th month. I put it off on the ground of excitement.

The Consolation of Conscience

Dear brother, I have no hopes of getting clear of being convicted and sentenced to the Penitentiary; but do not think that I am without comfort in my afflictions, for I assure thee that I have many reflections that give me sweet consolation in the midst of my grief. I have a clear conscience before my God, which is my greatest comfort and support through all my troubles and afflictions. An approving conscience none can know but those who enjoy it. It nerves us in the hour of trial to bear our sufferings with fortitude and even with cheerfulness. The greatest affliction I have is the reflection of the sorrow and anxiety my friends will have to endure on my account. But I can assure thee, brother, that, with the exception of this reflection, I am far, very far, from being one of the most miserable of men. Nay, to the contrary, I am not terrified at the prospect before me, though I am grieved about it; but all have enough to grieve about in this unfriendly wilderness of sin and woe. My hopes are not fixed in this world, and therefore I have a source of consolation that will never fail me, so long as I slight not the offers of mercy, comfort, and peace, which my blessed Saviour constantly privileges me with. . . .

Words to His Fiancée

Richard was engaged to a young lady of amiable disposition and fine mental endowments.

To her he thus writes:

Oh, dearest! Canst thou upbraid me? canst thou call it crime? wouldst thou call it crime, or couldst thou upbraid me, for rescuing, or attempting to rescue, *thy* father, mother, or brother and sister, or even friends, from a captivity among a cruel race of oppressors? Oh, couldst thou only see what I have seen, and hear what I have heard, of the sad, vexatious, degrading, and soul-trying situation of as noble minds as ever the Anglo-Saxon race were possessed of, mourning in vain for that universal heaven-born boon of freedom which an all-wise and beneficent Creator has designed for all, thou couldst not censure, but wouldst deeply sympathise with me! Take all these things into consideration, and the thousands of poor mortals who are dragging out far more miserable lives than mine will be, even at ten years in the Penitentiary, and thou wilt not look upon my fate with so much horror as thou would at first thought.

In another letter he adds:—

Have happy hours here, and I should not be miserable if I could only know you were not sorrowing for me at home. It would give me more satisfaction to hear that you were not grieving about me than anything else.

The nearer I live to the principle of the commandment, "Love thy neighbour as thyself," the more enjoyment I have of this life. None can know the enjoyments that flow from feelings of good-will towards our fellow-beings, both friends and enemies, but those who cultivate them. Even in my prison-cell I may be happy, if I will. For the Christian's consolation cannot be shut out from him by enemies or iron gates. . . .

Dillingham Goes on Trial

In another place he says, in view of his nearly approaching trial:

> O dear parents! The principles of love for my fellow-beings which you have instilled into my mind are some of the greatest consolations I have in my imprisonment, and they give me resignation to bear whatever may be inflicted upon me without feeling any malice or bitterness toward my vigilant prosecutors. If they show me mercy, it will be accepted by me with gratitude; but if they do not, I will endeavour to bear whatever they may inflict with Christian fortitude and resignation, and try not to murmur at my lot; but it is hard to obey the commandment, "Love your enemies."

The day of his trial at length came.

His youth, his engaging manners, frank address, and in-

Helping a Fugitive

Henry David Thoreau, one of the most influential American writers and philosophers, was also a committed abolitionist. Like many of his fellow abolitionist writers, Thoreau viewed his opposition to slavery as a matter requiring action as well as words. In the following brief excerpt from his journal dated October 1, 1851, Thoreau describes his own role in the local Underground Railroad. Thoreau offered the runaway, Henry Williams, a temporary haven where he could elude Boston police and await additional funds forwarded along by other Railroad operators to help him on his journey to Canada.

5 P.M. just put a fugitive slave who has taken the name of Henry Williams into the cars [the train] for Canada. He escaped from Stafford County Virginia to Boston last October, has been in Shadrack's place [Shadrack Minkins, a fugitive slave rescued from his captors in Boston] at the Cornhill Coffee-house—had been corresponding through an agent with his master who is his father about buying himself—his master asking $600 but he having been able to raise only $500—heard that there were writs out [arrest warrants] for two Williamses fugitives—and was informed by his fellow

variable gentleness to all who approached him, had won many friends, and the trial excited much interest.

His mother and her brother, Asa Williams, went a distance of 750 miles to attend his trial. They carried with them a certificate of his character, drawn up by Dr. Brisbane, and numerously signed by his friends and acquaintances, and officially countersigned by civil officers. This was done at the suggestion of his counsel, and exhibited by them in court. When brought to the bar it is said that "his demeanour was calm, dignified, and manly." His mother sat by his side. The prosecuting attorney waived his plea, and left the ground clear for Richard's counsel. Their defence was eloquent and pathetic. After they closed, Richard rose, and in a calm and dignified manner spoke extemporaneously as follows:

---

servants & employer that Augerhole Bums & others of the [Boston] police had called for him when he was out. Accordingly fled to Concord last night on foot—bringing a letter to our family from Mr [Owen] Lovejoy of Cambridge—& another which [abolitionist publisher William Lloyd] Garrison had formerly given him on another occasion.

He lodged with us & waited in the house till funds were collected with which to forward him. Intended to despatch him at noon through to Burlington—but when I went to buy his ticket saw one at the Depot [train station] who looked & behaved so much like a Boston policeman, that I did not venture that time.

An intelligent and very well behaved man—a mullatto. . . . The slave said he could guide himself by many other stars than the north star whose rising & setting he knew—They steered for the north star even when it had got round and appeared to them to be in the south. They frequently followed the telegraph when there was no railroad. The slaves bring many superstitions from Africa. The fugitives sometimes superstitiously carry a turf [a piece of soil] in their hats thinking that their success depends on it.

Henry David Thoreau, *A Year in Thoreau's Journal: 1851*. New York: Penguin, 1993.

By the kind permission of the court, for which I am sincerely thankful, I avail myself of the privilege of adding a few words to the remarks already made by my counsel. And although I stand, by my own confession, as a criminal in the eyes of your violated laws, yet I feel confident that I am addressing those who have hearts to feel; and in meting out the punishment that I am about to suffer, I hope you will be lenient; for it is a new situation in which I am placed. Never before, in the whole course of my life, have I been charged with a dishonest act. And from my childhood, kind parents, whose names I deeply reverence, have instilled into my mind a desire to be virtuous and honourable; and it has ever been my aim so to conduct myself as to merit the confidence and esteem of my fellow-men. But, gentlemen, I have violated your laws. This offence I did commit; and I now stand before you, to my sorrow and regret, as a criminal. But I was prompted to it by feelings of humanity. It has been suspected, as I was informed, that I am leagued with a fraternity who are combined for the purpose of committing such offences as the one with which I am charged. But gentlemen, the impression is false. I alone am guilty—I alone committed the offence—and I alone must suffer the penalty. My parents, my friends, my relatives, are as innocent of any participation in or knowledge of my offence as the babe unborn. My parents are still living, though advanced in years, and, in the course of nature, a few more years will terminate their earthly existence. In their old age and infirmity they will need a stay and protection; and, if you can, consistently with your ideas of justice, make my term of imprisonment a short one, you will receive the lasting gratitude of a son who reverences his parents, and the prayers and blessings of an aged father and mother who love their child.

Verdict and Sentence

A great deal of sensation now appeared in the court-room, and most of the jury are said to have wept. They retired for a few moments, and returned a verdict for three years' imprisonment in the Penitentiary.

The *Nashville Daily Gazette* of April 13, 1849, contains the following notice:

THE KIDNAPPING CASE

Richard Dillingham, who was arrested on the 5th day of September last, having in his possession three slaves, whom he intended to convey with him to a free state, was arraigned yesterday and tried in the criminal court. The prisoner confessed his guilt, and made a short speech in palliation of his offence. He avowed that the act was undertaken by himself without instigation from any source, and he alone was responsible for the error into which his education had led him. He had, he said, no other motive than the good of the slaves, and did not expect to claim any advantage by freeing them. He was sentenced to three years' imprisonment in the penitentiary, the least time the law allows for the offence committed. Mr. Dillingham is a Quaker from Ohio, and has been a teacher in that State. He belongs to a respectable family, and he is not without the sympathy of those who attended the trial. It was a fool-hardy enterprise in which he embarked, and dearly has he paid for his rashness.

An Appeal to the Governor

His mother, before leaving Nashville, visited the governor, and had an interview with him in regard to pardoning her son. He gave her some encouragement, but thought she had better postpone her petition for the present. After the lapse of several months, she wrote to him about it; but he seemed to have changed his mind, as the following letter will show:

Nashville
August 29, 1849

Dear Madam,

Your letter of the 6th of the 7th mo. was received, and would have been noticed earlier but for my absence from home. Your solicitude for your son is natural, and it would be gratifying to be able to reward it by releasing him, if it were in my power. But the offence for which he is suffering was clearly made out, and its tendency here is very hurtful to our rights, and our peace as a people. He is doomed to the shortest period known to our statute. And, at all events, I could not interfere with his case for some time to come; and, to be frank with you, I do not see how his time can be lessened at all. But my term of office will expire soon, and the Governor elect, Gen. William Trousdale, will take my place. To him you will make any future appeal.

Yours, &c., N.L. Brown.

. . . Dillingham had been in prison little more than a year when the cholera invaded Nashville, and broke out among the inmates; Richard was up day and night in attendance on the sick, his disinterested and sympathetic nature leading him to labours to which his delicate constitution, impaired by confinement, was altogether inadequate. . . .

Worn with these labours, the gentle, patient lover of God and of his brother sank at last overwearied, and passed peacefully away to a world where all are lovely and loving.

Though his correspondence with her he most loved was interrupted, from his unwillingness to subject his letters to the surveillance of the warden, yet a note reached her, conveyed through the hands of a prisoner whose time was out. In this letter, the last which any earthly friend ever received, he says: "I oft-times, yea, *all* times, think of thee; if I did not, I should cease to exist."

What must that system be which makes it necessary to imprison with convicted felons a man like this, because he loves his brother man, "not wisely but too well?"

Chapter 5

Obstacles
to Freedom

Chapter Preface

P art of the Compromise of 1850 that admitted California to the Union as a free state but designated slavery in the territories a matter for their particular populaces to decide, the new Fugitive Slave Act empowered federal officers to apprehend runaways, denied alleged fugitives basic due-process rights, and not only stiffened penalties for those abetting refugees, but also required that citizens actively assist in their recapture. The new law was designed to placate Southerners who were displeased with the other terms of the Compromise and to effectively nullify the 1842 U.S. Supreme Court decision in *Prigg v. Pennsylvania*. In *Prigg* the Court had ruled that Edward Prigg, the agent of a Maryland slave owner, could be lawfully convicted of kidnapping under Pennsylvania law for attempting to seize the fugitive bondwoman, Margaret Morgan, in Pennsylvania, a free state. The Court's decision essentially invalidated the 1793 federal fugitive slave statute by holding that its enforcement, while licit, did not preclude sovereign states from enforcing their own laws.

Yet in the aftermath of the 1850 Fugitive Slave Act there is scant evidence that private citizens in the North actively cooperated with authorities in apprehending runaways. To the contrary, countless Northerners not previously involved in the abolitionist movement strove to intervene when federal officers or bounty hunters seized a fugitive, occasionally leading to the eruption of riots and violent confrontations. The Fugitive Slave Act's widespread unpopularity notwithstanding, many refugees were captured and returned to slavery, and many of those attempting to assist them were charged, fined, and even imprisoned, such as Sherman Booth in the Joshua Glover case in Racine, Wisconsin, and Charles Langston and Simeon Bushnell in the Oberlin-Wellington rescue, in which a rioting crowd descended upon an inn to free by force a runaway named John Price.

The Fugitive Slave Act

U.S. Congress

The Fugitive Slave Act was part of the Compromise of 1850, a body of legislation designed to placate both the proslavery South and an increasingly antislavery North. Instead, the compromise, especially the Fugitive Slave Act, served to fan the flames of sectional discord. The compromise's major components were the admission of California as a free state, and, to pacify the slave interests who favored allowing slavery's westward expansion, a new, more stringent Fugitive Slave Act to supersede the existing 1793 version.

For nearly two decades Southern politicians had been hotly complaining about the perceived interference and "agitation" of abolitionists with a legal institution. They accused antislavery activists of inciting slaves to rebel and run away, of flooding the South with abolitionist propaganda, whether through the words of pamphlets or itinerant preachers. The new Fugitive Slave Act specifically criminalized the act of abetting runaway slaves even in the free states, mandating stiff fines for those convicted of the federal offense. Moreover, the new law denied accused runways of even the semblance of due process, including the rights to stage a defense and to a jury trial, which jeopardized free blacks as well as fugitives. In response, many prominent black abolitionists fled to England, including William Wells Brown, Henry "Box" Brown, and William and Ellen Craft. More and more fugitives chose Canada as their only safe destination on the

U.S. Congress, Fugitive Slave Act, September 18, 1850.

continent. The antislavery community as a whole denounced the law and urged civil disobedience.

Section 1: Be it enacted by the Senate and House of Representatives of the United States of America in Congress assembled, That the persons who have been, or may hereafter be, appointed commissioners, in virtue of any act of Congress, by the Circuit Courts of the United States, and Who, in consequence of such appointment, are authorized to exercise the powers that any justice of the peace, or other magistrate of any of the United States, may exercise in respect to offenders for any crime or offense against the United States, by arresting, imprisoning, or bailing the same under and by the virtue of the thirty-third section of the act of the twenty-fourth of September seventeen hundred and eighty-nine, entitled "An Act to establish the judicial courts of the United States" shall be, and are hereby, authorized and required to exercise and discharge all the powers and duties conferred by this act.

Section 2: And be it further enacted, That the Superior Court of each organized Territory of the United States shall have the same power to appoint commissioners to take acknowledgments of bail and affidavits, and to take depositions of witnesses in civil causes, which is now possessed by the Circuit Court of the United States; and all commissioners who shall hereafter be appointed for such purposes by the Superior Court of any organized Territory of the United States, shall possess all the powers, and exercise all the duties, conferred by law upon the commissioners appointed by the Circuit Courts of the United States for similar purposes, and shall moreover exercise and discharge all the powers and duties conferred by this act.

Section 3: And be it further enacted, That the Circuit Courts of the United States shall from time to time enlarge the number of the commissioners, with a view to afford reasonable facilities to reclaim fugitives from labor, and to the prompt discharge of the duties imposed by this act.

Section 4: And be it further enacted, That the commissioners above named shall have concurrent jurisdiction with the judges of the Circuit and District Courts of the United States, in their respective circuits and districts within the several States, and the judges of the Superior Courts of the Territories, severally and collectively, in term-time and vacation; shall grant certificates to such claimants, upon satisfactory proof being made, with authority to take and remove such fugitives from service or labor, under the restrictions herein contained, to the State or Territory from which such persons may have escaped or fled.

Law Officers Must Comply

Section 5: And be it further enacted, That it shall be the duty of all marshals and deputy marshals to obey and execute all warrants and precepts issued under the provisions of this act, when to them directed; and should any marshal or deputy marshal refuse to receive such warrant, or other process, when tendered, or to use all proper means diligently to execute the same, he shall, on conviction thereof, be fined in the sum of one thousand dollars, to the use of such claimant, on the motion of such claimant, by the Circuit or District Court for the district of such marshal; and after arrest of such fugitive, by such marshal or his deputy, or whilst at any time in his custody under the provisions of this act, should such fugitive escape, whether with or without the assent of such marshal or his deputy, such marshal shall be liable, on his official bond, to be prosecuted for the benefit of such claimant, for the full value of the service or labor of said fugitive in the State, Territory, or District whence he escaped: and the better to enable the said commissioners, when thus appointed, to execute their duties faithfully and efficiently, in conformity with the requirements of the Constitution of the United States and of this act, they are hereby authorized and empowered, within their counties respectively, to appoint, in writing under their hands, any one or more suitable persons, from time to time, to execute all such warrants and other process as may be issued by them in the

lawful performance of their respective duties; with authority to such commissioners, or the persons to be appointed
by them, to execute process as aforesaid, to summon and
call to their aid the bystanders, or posse comitatus of the
proper county, when necessary to ensure a faithful obser-
vance of the clause of the Constitution referred to, in conformity with the provisions of this act; and all good citizens
are hereby commanded to aid and assist in the prompt and
efficient execution of this law, whenever their services may
be required, as aforesaid, for that purpose; and said warrants
shall run, and be executed by said officers, any where in the
State within which they are issued.

The Right to Reclaim Fugitives

Section 6: And be it further enacted, That when a person
held to service or labor in any State or Territory of the
United States, has heretofore or shall hereafter escape into
another State or Territory of the United States, the person or
persons to whom such service or labor may be due, or his,
her, or their agent or attorney, duly authorized, by power of
attorney, in writing, acknowledged and certified under the
seal of some legal officer or court of the State or Territory
in which the same may be executed, may pursue and reclaim
such fugitive person, either by procuring a warrant from
some one of the courts, judges, or commissioners aforesaid,
of the proper circuit, district, or county, for the apprehension of such fugitive from service or labor, or by seizing and
arresting such fugitive, where the same can be done without
process, and by taking, or causing such person to be taken,
forthwith before such court, judge, or commissioner, whose
duty it shall be to hear and determine the case of such
claimant in a summary manner; and upon satisfactory proof
being made, by deposition or affidavit, in writing, to be
taken and certified by such court, judge, or commissioner,
or by other satisfactory testimony, duly taken and certified
by some court, magistrate, justice of the peace, or other legal officer authorized to administer an oath and take depositions under the laws of the State or Territory from which

such person owing service or labor may have escaped, with a certificate of such magistracy or other authority, as aforesaid, with the seal of the proper court or officer thereto attached, which seal shall be sufficient to establish the competency of the proof, and with proof, also by affidavit, of the identity of the person whose service or labor is claimed to be due as aforesaid, that the person so arrested does in fact owe service or labor to the person or persons claiming him or her, in the State or Territory from which such fugitive may have escaped as aforesaid, and that said person escaped, to make out and deliver to such claimant, his or her agent or attorney, a certificate setting forth the substantial facts as to the service or labor due from such fugitive to the

The Proper Response to the Fugitive Slave Act

Abolitionists reacted to the Fugitive Slave Act of 1850 with widespread anger and outrage. In the following excerpt from an editorial in his newspaper, Frederick Douglass, who had previously discouraged violent resistance, proposed what he called "The True Remedy for the Fugitive Slave Bill"—armed opposition both to the new law and to the institution of slavery itself.

A good revolver, a steady hand, and a determination to shoot down any man attempting to kidnap *[that is, arrest or capture fugitive slaves].* Let every colored man make up his mind to this, and live by it, and if needs be, die by it. This will put an end to kidnapping and to slaveholding, too. We blush to our very soul when we are told that a negro is so mean and cowardly that he prefers to live under the slave driver's whip—to the loss of life for liberty. Oh! that we had a little more of the manly indifference to death, which characterized the Heroes of the American Revolution.

Frederick Douglass's Paper, Rochester, New York, June 9, 1854.

claimant, and of his or her escape from the State or Territory in which he or she was arrested, with authority to such claimant, or his or her agent or attorney, to use such reasonable force and restraint as may be necessary, under the circumstances of the case, to take and remove such fugitive person back to the State or Territory whence he or she may have escaped as aforesaid. In no trial or hearing under this act shall the testimony of such alleged fugitive be admitted in evidence; and the certificates in this and the first [fourth] section mentioned, shall be conclusive of the right of the person or persons in whose favor granted, to remove such fugitive to the State or Territory from which he escaped, and shall prevent all molestation of such person or persons by any process issued by any court, judge, magistrate, or other person whomsoever.

Abettors Will Be Punished

Section 7: And be it further enacted, That any person who shall knowingly and willingly obstruct, hinder, or prevent such claimant, his agent or attorney, or any person or persons lawfully assisting him, her, or them, from arresting such a fugitive from service or labor, either with or without process as aforesaid, or shall rescue, or attempt to rescue, such fugitive from service or labor, from the custody of such claimant, his or her agent or attorney, or other person or persons lawfully assisting as aforesaid, when so arrested, pursuant to the authority herein given and declared; or shall aid, abet, or assist such person so owing service or labor as aforesaid, directly or indirectly, to escape from such claimant, his agent or attorney, or other person or persons legally authorized as aforesaid; or shall harbor or conceal such fugitive, so as to prevent the discovery and arrest of such person, after notice or knowledge of the fact that such person was a fugitive from service or labor as aforesaid, shall, for either of said offences, be subject to a fine not exceeding one thousand dollars, and imprisonment not exceeding six months, by indictment and conviction before the District Court of the United States for the district in which such offence may have been committed, or before the proper court of criminal jurisdiction, if committed within any one of the organized Territories of the United States; and shall moreover forfeit and pay, by way of civil damages to the party injured by such illegal conduct, the sum of one thousand dollars for each fugitive so lost as aforesaid, to be recovered by action of debt, in any of the District or Territorial Courts aforesaid, within whose jurisdiction the said offence may have been committed.

Payment for Aiding an Arrest

Section 8: And be it further enacted, That the marshals, their deputies, and the clerks of the said District and Territorial Courts, shall be paid, for their services, the like fees as may be allowed for similar services in other cases; and where such services are rendered exclusively in the arrest, custody, and delivery of the fugitive to the claimant, his or her agent or attorney, or where such supposed fugitive may be discharged out of custody for the want of sufficient proof as aforesaid, then such fees are to be paid in whole by such claimant, his or her agent or attorney; and in all cases where the proceedings are before a commissioner, he shall be entitled to a fee of ten dollars in full for his services in each case, upon the delivery of the said certificate to the claimant, his agent or attorney; or a fee of five dollars in cases where the proof shall not, in the opinion of such commissioner, warrant such certificate and delivery, inclusive of all services incident to such arrest and examination, to be paid, in either case, by the claimant, his or her agent or attorney. The person or persons authorized to execute the process to be issued by such commissioner for the arrest and detention of fugitives from service or labor as aforesaid, shall also be entitled to a fee of five dollars each for each person he or they may arrest, and take before any commissioner as aforesaid, at the instance and request of such claimant, with such other fees as may be deemed reasonable by such commissioner for such other additional services as may be necessarily performed by him or them; such as attending at the examination, keeping the fugitive in custody, and providing him with food and lodging during his detention, and until the final determination of such commissioners; and, in general, for performing such other duties as may be required by such claimant, his or her attorney or agent, or commissioner in the premises, such fees to be made up in conformity with the fees usually charged by the officers of the courts of justice within the proper district or county, as near as may be practicable, and paid by such claimants, their agents or attorneys, whether such supposed fugitives from service or labor be ordered to be delivered to such claimant by the final determination of such commissioner or not.

Section 9: And be it further enacted, That, upon affidavit made by the claimant of such fugitive, his agent or attorney, after such certificate has been issued, that he has reason to apprehend that such fugitive will be rescued by force from his or their possession before he can be taken beyond the limits of the State in which the arrest is made, it shall be the duty of the officer making the arrest to retain such fugitive in his custody, and to remove him to the State whence he fled, and there to deliver him to said claimant, his agent, or attorney. And to this end, the officer aforesaid is hereby authorized and required to employ so many persons as he may deem necessary to overcome such force, and to retain them in his service so long as circumstances may require. The said officer and his assistants, while so employed, to receive the same compensation, and to be allowed the same expenses, as are now allowed by law for transportation of criminals, to be certified by the judge of the district within which the arrest is made, and paid out of the treasury of the United States.

Proof of Ownership

Section 10: And be it further enacted, That when any person held to service or labor in any State or Territory, or in the District of Columbia, shall escape therefrom, the party to whom such service or labor shall be due, his, her, or their agent or attorney, may apply to any court of record therein, or judge thereof in vacation, and make satisfactory proof to such court, or judge in vacation, of the escape aforesaid, and that the person escaping owed service or labor to such party. Whereupon the court shall cause a record to be made of the matters so proved, and also a general description of the person so escaping, with such convenient certainty as may be; and a transcript of such record, authenticated by the attestation of the clerk and of the seal of the said court, being produced in any other State, Territory, or district in which the person so escaping may be found, and being exhibited to any judge, commissioner, or other office, authorized by the law of the United States to cause persons escaping from service or labor to be delivered up, shall be held and taken to be full and conclusive evidence of the fact of escape, and that the service or labor of the person escaping is due to the party in such record mentioned. And upon the production by the said party of other and further evidence if necessary, either oral or by affidavit, in addition to what is contained in the said record of the identity of the person escaping, he or she shall be delivered up to the claimant, And the said court, commissioner, judge, or other person authorized by this act to grant certificates to claimants or fugitives, shall, upon the production of the record and other evidences aforesaid, grant to such claimant a certificate of his right to take any such person identified and proved to be owing service or labor as aforesaid, which certificate shall authorize such claimant to seize or arrest and transport such person to the State or Territory from which he escaped: Provided, That nothing herein contained shall be construed as requiring the production of a transcript of such record as evidence as aforesaid. But in its absence the claim shall be heard and determined upon other satisfactory proofs, competent in law.

The Fugitive Slave Act Is Just

Daniel Webster

Statesman, lawyer, and famed orator, Daniel Webster served both New Hampshire and Massachusetts in the U.S. Congress. Webster was also twice secretary of state, first under William Henry Harrison and later under Millard Fillmore. During his latter term as secretary of state, he meticulously oversaw the implementation of the Fugitive Slave Act, incurring the wrath of New England's many vocal abolitionists, such as Henry David Thoreau and William Lloyd Garrison.

Like many members of the Whig Party, Webster opposed the westward expansion of slavery, supporting the Compromise of 1850 that admitted California into the Union as a free state but radically reformed the existing Fugitive Slave Act to target individuals who assisted runaways along with the fugitives themselves. In his famous speech of March 7, 1850, before the U.S. Congress, excerpted in the following selection, Webster urges the North to comply with the Fugitive Slave Act for the good of a national unity increasingly taxed by the conflict over slavery. Although Webster grants the legitimacy of both the Northern and Southern position on slavery, he seems to give more weight to the grievances of slave interests, characterizing abolitionists as sincere but troublemaking instigators in the conflict. But Webster saves his most passionate words to decry the very notion of Southern secession over the slavery dispute, a possibility he and many other Whigs hoped to preclude with the new Fugitive Slave Act.

Daniel Webster, address to the U.S. Congress, March 7, 1850.

M r. President, I wish to speak today, not as a Massachusetts man, nor as a Northern man, but as an American, and a member of the Senate of the United States. It is fortunate that there is a Senate of the United States; a body not yet moved from its propriety, not lost to a just sense of its own dignity and its own high responsibilities, and a body to which the country looks, with confidence, for wise, moderate, patriotic, and healing counsels. It is not to be denied that we live in the midst of strong agitations, and are surrounded by very considerable dangers to our institutions and our government. The imprisoned winds are let loose. The East, the North, and the stormy South combine to throw the whole sea into commotion, to toss its billows to the skies, and disclose its profoundest depths. I do not affect to regard myself, Mr. President, as holding, or as fit to hold, the helm in this combat with the political elements; but I have a duty to perform, and I mean to perform it with fidelity, not without a sense of existing dangers, but not without hope. I have a part to act, not for my own security or safety, for I am looking out for no fragment upon which to float away from the wreck, if wreck there must be, but for the good of the whole, and the preservation of all; and there is that which will keep me to my duty during this struggle, whether the sun and the stars shall appear, or shall not appear for many days. I speak today for the preservation of the Union. "Hear me for my cause." I speak today, out of a solicitous and anxious heart for the restoration to the country of that quiet and harmonious harmony which make the blessings of this Union so rich, and so dear to us all. These are the topics I propose to myself to discuss; these are the motives, and the sole motives, that influence me in the wish to communicate my opinions to the Senate and the country; and if I can do any thing, however little, for the promotion of these ends, I shall have accomplished all that I expect . . .

Sectional Differences over Slavery

Now, Sir, upon the general nature and influence of slavery there exists a wide difference of opinion between the northern portion of this country and the southern. It is said on the one side, that, although not the subject of any injunction or direct prohibition in the New Testament, slavery is a wrong; that it is founded merely in the right of the strongest; and that is an oppression, like unjust wars, like all those conflicts by which a powerful nation subjects a weaker to its will; and that, in its nature, whatever may be said of it in the modifications which have taken place, it is not according to the meek spirit of the Gospel. It is not "kindly affectioned"; it does not "seek another's, and not its own"; it does not "let the oppressed go free". These are the sentiments that are cherished, and of late with greatly augmented force, among the people of the Northern States. They have taken hold of the religious sentiment of that part of the country, as they have, more or less, taken hold of the religious feeling of a considerable portion of mankind. The South, upon the other side, having been accustomed to this relation between two races all their lives, from their birth, having been taught, in general, to treat the subjects of this bondage with care and kindness, and I believe, in general, feeling great kindness for them, have not taken the view of the subject which I have mentioned. There are thousands of religious men, with consciences as tender as any of their brethren at the North, who do not see the unlawfulness of slavery; and there are more thousands, perhaps, that whatsoever they may think of it in its origin, and as a matter depending upon natural right, yet take things as they are, and, finding slavery to be an established relation of the society in which they live, can see no way in which, let their opinions on the abstract question be what they may, it is in the power of the present generation to relieve themselves from this relation. And candor obliges me to say, that I believe they are just as conscientious, many of them, and the religious people, all of them, as they are at the North who hold different opinions.

Religious Beliefs in Conflict

The honorable Senator from South Carolina [John C. Calhoun] the other day alluded to the separation of that great religious community, the Methodist Episcopal Church. That separation was brought about by differences of opinion upon this particular subject of slavery. I felt great concern, as that dispute went on, about the result. I was in hopes that the difference of opinion might be adjusted, because I looked upon that religious denomination as one of the great props of religion and morals throughout the whole country, from Maine to Georgia, and westward to our utmost boundary. The result was against my wishes and against my hopes. I have read all their proceedings and all their arguments; but I have never yet been able to come to the conclusion that there was any real ground for that separation; in other words, that any good could be produced by that separation. I must say I think there was some want of candor or charity. Sir, when a question of this kind seizes on the religious sentiments of mankind, and comes to be discussed in religious assemblies of the clergy and laity, there is always to be expected, or always to be feared, a great degree of excitement. It is in the nature of man, manifested in his whole history, that religious disputes are apt to become warm in proportion to the strength of the convictions which men entertain of the magnitude of the questions at issue. In all such disputes, there will sometimes be found men with whom every thing is absolute; absolutely wrong, or absolutely right. They see the right clearly; they think others ought so to see it, and they are disposed to establish a broad line of distinction between what is right and what is wrong. They are not seldom willing to establish that line upon their own convictions of truth or justice; and are ready to mark and guard it by placing along it a series of dogmas, as lines of boundary on the earth's surface are marked by posts and stones. There are men who, with clear perception, as they think, of their own duty, do not see how too eager a pursuit of one duty may involve them in the violation of others, or how too warm an embracement of one truth may lead to a disregard of other truths equally important. As I heard it stated strongly, not many days ago, these persons are disposed to mount upon some particular duty, as upon a war-horse, and to drive furiously on and upon and over all other duties that may stand in the way. There are men who, in reference to disputes of that sort, are of the opinion that human duties may be ascertained with the exactness of mathematics. They deal with morals as with mathematics; and they think what is right may be distinguished from what is wrong with the precision of an algebraic equation. They have, therefore, none too much charity towards others who differ from them. They are apt, too, to think that nothing is good but what is perfect, and that there are no compromises or modifications to be made in consideration of difference of opinion or in deference to other men's judgment. If their perspicacious vision enables them to detect a spot on the face of the sun, they think that a good reason why the sun should be struck down from heaven. They prefer the chance of running into utter darkness to living in heavenly light, if that heavenly light be not absolutely without any imperfection. There are impatient men; too impatient always to give heed to the admonition of St. Paul, that we are not to "do evil that good may come"; too impatient to wait for the slow progress of moral causes in the improvement of mankind . . .

The North Is Bound to Deliver Up Fugitives

Mr. President, in the excited times in which we live, there is found to exist a state of crimination and recrimination between the North and South. There are lists of grievances produced by each; and those grievances, real or supposed, alienate the minds of one portion of the country from the other, exasperate the feelings, and subdue the sense of fraternal affection, patriotic love, and mutual regard. I shall bestow a little attention, Sir, upon these various grievances existing on the one side and on the other. I begin with complaints of the South. I will not answer, further than I have, the general statements of the honorable Senator from South Carolina [Calhoun], that the North has prospered at the expense of the South in consequence of the manner of administering this government, in the collecting of its revenues, and so forth. These are disputed topics, and I have no inclination to enter into them. But I will allude to the other complaints of the South, and especially to one which has in my opinion just foundation; and that is, that there has been found at the North, among individuals and among legislators, a disinclination to perform fully their constitutional duties in regard to the return of persons bound to service who have escaped into the free States. In that respect, the South, in my judgment, is right, and the North is wrong. Every member of every Northern legislature is bound by oath, like every other officer in the country, to support the Constitution of the United States; and the article of the Constitution which says to these States that they shall deliver up fugitives from service is as binding in honor and conscience as any other article. No man fulfills his duty in any legislature who sets himself to find excuses, evasions, escapes from this constitutional obligation. I have always thought that the Constitution addressed itself to the legislatures of the States or to the States themselves. It says that those persons es-

A runaway slave is captured after trying to escape to a free state. The Fugitive Slave Act required Northerners to return the slaves to their owners.

caping to other States "shall be delivered up," and I confess I have always been of the opinion that it was an injunction upon the States themselves. When it is said that a person escaping into another State, and coming therefore within the jurisdiction of that State, shall be delivered up, it seems to me the import of the clause is, that the State itself, in obedience to the Constitution, shall cause him to be delivered up. That is my judgment. I have always entertained that opinion, and I entertain it now. But when the subject, some years ago, was before the Supreme Court of the United States, the majority of the judges held that the power to cause fugitives from service to be delivered up was a power to be exercised under the authority of this government. I do not know, on the whole, that it may not have been a fortunate decision. My habit is to respect the result of judicial deliberations and the solemnity of judicial decisions. As it now stands, the business of seeing that these fugitives are delivered up resides in the power of Congress and the national judicature, and my friend at the head of the Judiciary Committee [James M. Mason] has a bill on the subject now before the Senate, which, with some amendments to it, I propose to support, with all its provisions, to the fullest extent. And I desire to call the attention of all sober-minded men at the North, of all conscientious men, of all men who are not carried away by some fanatical idea or some false impression, to their constitutional obligations. I put it to all the sober and sound minds at the North as a question of morals and a question of conscience. What right have they, in their legislative capacity or any other capacity, to endeavor to get round this Constitution, or to embarrass the free exercise of the rights secured by the Constitution to the persons whose slaves escape from them? None at all; none at all. Neither in the forum of conscience, nor before the face of the Constitution, are they, in my opinion, justified in such an attempt. Of course it is a matter for their consideration. They probably, in the excitement of the times, have not stopped to consider of this. They have followed what seemed to be the current of thought and of motives, as the occasion arose, and they have neglected to investigate fully the real question, and to consider their constitutional obligations; which, I am sure, if they did consider, they would fulfill with alacrity. I repeat, therefore, Sir, that here is a well-founded ground of complaint against the North, which ought to be removed, which it is now in the power of the different departments of this government to remove; which calls for the enactment of proper laws authorizing the judicature of this government, in the several States, to do all that is necessary for the recapture of fugitive slaves and for their restoration to those who claim them. Wherever I go, and whenever I speak on the subject, and when I speak here I desire to speak to the whole North, I say that the South has been injured in this respect, and has a right to complain; and the North has been too careless of what I think the Constitution peremptorily and emphatically enjoins upon her as a duty . . .

Abolitionist Agitation

Then, Sir, there are the Abolition societies, of which I am unwilling to speak, but in regard to which I have very clear notions and opinions. I do not think them useful. I think their operations for the last twenty years have produced nothing good or valuable. At the same time, I believe thousands of their members to be honest and good men, perfectly well-meaning men. They have excited feelings; they think they must do something for the cause of liberty; and, in their sphere of action, they do not see what else they can do than to contribute to an Abolition press, or an Abolition society, or to pay an Abolition lecturer. I do not mean to impute gross motives even to the leaders of these societies, but I am not blind to the consequences of their proceedings. I cannot but see what mischiefs their interference with the South has produced. And is it not plain to every man? Let any gentleman who entertains doubts on this point recur to the debates in the Virginia House of Delegates in 1832, and he will see with what freedom a proposition made by Mr. [Thomas] Jefferson Randolph for the gradual abolition of slavery was discussed in that body. Every one spoke of slavery as he thought; very ignominious and disparaging names and epithets were applied to it. The debates in the House of Delegates on that occasion, I believe, were all published. They were read by every colored man who could read, and to those who could not read, those debates were read by others. At that time Virginia was not unwilling or unafraid to discuss this question, and to let that part of her population know as much of [that] discussion as they could learn. That was in 1832. As has been said by the honorable member from South Carolina [Calhoun], these Abolition societies commenced their course of action in 1835. It is said, I do not know how true it may be, that they sent incendiary publications into the slave States; at any rate, they attempted to arouse, and did arouse, a very strong feeling; in other words, they created great agitation in the North against Southern slavery. Well, what was the result? The bonds of the slave were bound more firmly than before, their rivets were more strongly fastened. Public opinion, which in Virginia had begun to be exhibited against slavery, and was opening out for the discussion of the question, drew back and shut itself up in its castle. I wish to know whether any body in Virginia can now talk openly as Mr. Randoph, Governor [James] McDowell, and others talked in 1832 and sent their remarks to the press? We all know the fact, and we all know the cause; and every thing that these agitating people have done has been, not to enlarge, but to restrain, not to set free, but to bind faster the slave population of the South . . .

Secession Would Result in War

Mr. President, I should much prefer to have heard from every member on this floor declarations of opinion that this Union could never be dissolved, than the declaration of opinion by any body, that, in any case, under the pressure of any circumstances, such a dissolution was possible. I hear with distress and anguish the word "secession," especially when it falls from the lips of those who are patriotic, and known to the country, and known all over the world, for their political services. Secession! Peaceable secession! Sir, your eyes and mine are never destined to see that miracle. The dismemberment of this vast country without convulsion! The breaking up of the fountains of the great deep without ruffling the surface! Who is so foolish, I beg every body's pardon, as to expect to see any such thing? Sir, he who sees these States, now revolving in harmony around a common center, and expects to see them quit their places and fly off without convulsion, may look the next hour to see heavenly bodies rush from their spheres, and jostle against each other in the realms of space, without causing the wreck of the universe. There can be no such thing as peaceable secession. Peaceable secession is an utter impossibility. Is the great Constitution under which we live, covering this whole country, is it to be thawed and melted away by secession, as the snows on the mountain melt under the influence of a vernal sun, disappear almost unobserved, and run off? No, Sir! No, Sir! I will not state what might produce the disruption of the Union; but, Sir, I see as plainly as I see the sun in heaven what that disruption itself must produce; I see that it must produce war, and such a war as I will not describe, *in its twofold character.*

A Fugitive Seems to Recant

Buffalo Commercial Advertiser, *Buffalo Morning Express*, and *New York Daily Tribune*

Throughout the heated sectional debate over slavery, defenders of the institution sought to counter the ever-proliferating popular slave narratives, with their wrenching accounts of human suffering, with claims that the vast majority of slaves were happy and well-cared for. According to the proslavery propaganda, slaves were simple, childlike souls whose inferior nature suited them only to bondage under benevolent white masters. This insistence on the "happy slave" was often accompanied by indictments of the far harsher living conditions endured by poor free laborers in the North. Slaveholders were fond of citing largely undocumented cases of runaway slaves choosing to return to their masters after getting a taste of freedom's false promises in the North.

The following selection is composed of newspaper reports of a highly publicized capture of a runaway slave named Daniel, the first such capture to take place in Buffalo, New York, after the enactment of the 1850 Fugitive Slave Act. The complicated case involved not only the apprehension of Daniel by the agent of his owner but also the runaway's charges that the agent, Mr. Rust, inflicted injuries upon him in the process of capture. What makes Daniel's case particularly remarkable is the appearance of a letter supposedly composed by the jailed fugitive in which the writer expresses regret for having run away from his kind master, extols the comforts of slave life, exhorts fellow bondsmen to stay where

Buffalo Commercial Advertiser, *Buffalo Morning Express*, and *New York Daily Tribune*, "Reform, Religion, and the Underground Railroad in Western New York," http://ublib.buffalo.edu, 2003.

they are, and implores abolitionists to interfere no further on his behalf. An obvious fabrication, the letter was roundly ridiculed, not the least because "Daniel" manages to touch upon so many of the key points characteristic of proslavery propaganda. The presiding judge freed Daniel, who, to the surprise of few, promptly continued along his way to Canada rather than returning to the supposedly idyllic life in Kentucky that he had fled.

Buffalo Commercial Advertiser
August 15, 1851

ARREST OF A FUGITIVE.

Deputy Marshall Gates this forenoon arrested the second cook of the steamer *Buckeye State*, on a charge of being "fugitive from service"—the agent or the owner, who resides in Louisville, KY., having made the necessary affidavits to obtain process, &c. The negro attempted to escape and received a severe blow upon his head. He was brought before U.S. Commissioner H.K. Smith, Esq., and the case is now undergoing investigation.

Quite a crowd gathered in front of Spaulding's Exchange, in which the office of the Commissioner is situated, but there was little or no excitement until an adjournment took place to the Court House. When the slave was taken to the carriage a rush was made by the negroes who followed it and stopped it once or twice.

Buffalo Commercial Advertiser
August 16, 1851

HOME MATTERS. THE FIRST FUGITIVE SLAVE CASE IN BUFFALO.

As we briefly announced yesterday, a fugitive slave was arrested on board the steamer *Buckeye State* yesterday forenoon, and the examination resulted in his being delivered up to the Agent of the owner.

The particulars of the arrest as we learn them are as follows:

Deputy Marshal Geo. B. Gates, Officer J.K. Tyler, Officer

Pierce with some others in company with Mr. Benj. S. Rust, the agent for the owner, Mr. George H. Moore, of Louisville, KY., proceeded with the necessary warrant to the dock at the foot of Commercial Street, where the *Buckeye State* was lying, and on board of which the fugitive Daniel was employed as second cook. Unlike all other lake steamers the kitchen on board this boat is below the main deck and is entered from the forward cabin below stairs, and has also an entrance by means of a small hatchway from the deck. Officer Tyler proceeded with the agent, Mr. Rust, through the cabin to the kitchen, where after Mr. R. had pointed out his man, he left the officer and returned on deck. Daniel, who is a very stout negro, refused to accompany the officer and with his four companions laid hold of their knives as if determined to show fight and threatened to "walk over corpses" if the arrest was made. Officer Tyler advised them to submit as he had not come there single handed and was bound to satisfy his warrant. He then sent for Marshal Gates and posse to come to his assistance and upon their approach Daniel dropped his knife and darted up the small hatch ladder to make his escape when his head came in violent contact with some substance—supposed to have been struck by some one on deck—causing him to fall back upon the stove. He was badly hurt and considerably burned but was then secured and taken.

After the arrest the slave Daniel was taken to the officer of the U.S. Commissioner, Hon. H.K. Smith, in Spaulding's Exchange. A large crowd—consisting principally of colored men—soon assembled, but all were very quiet and orderly. The Commissioner arrived at his office about 2 o'clock, when an adjournment took place to the Court House. As soon as the officers started for a carriage, a rush was made, and the excitement began. The crowd followed the carriage through Main Street, making demonstrations and uttering threats and impeded its course by taking hold of the wheels and horses but effected nothing further. There was considerable tumult in the street, and the colored people were much excited; and a few unprincipled white men attempted to increase the disturbance by inflammatory appeals. But the citizens, generally, were ready to stand by the officers in case of need and to vindicate the law and preserve the peace and character of the city.

The fugitive was taken to the court house, when the following proceedings were had:

Before Hon. H.K. Smith, U.S. Commissioner.

Case of the Negro man, Daniel, arrested on a warrant issuing on a record made in the County Court of Jefferson County, Kentucky.

For the Claimants, Foster and Bowen.

For the Defense, Talcott and Hawley.

Daniel was arrested on the steamer *Buckeye State*, yesterday morning, on board which vessel he was engaged as 2d cook. He is a fine, athletic negro, of great value, doubtless, to his owner. In the attempt to escape, he had fallen on the cooking stove in the kitchen, and when brought into the court, it was with a great burn upon his cheek and some severe contusions and flesh wounds about the head.

Defense claimed that the papers were insufficient, in that the record of the court in Kentucky was not properly sealed—the seal being impressed upon the record and not affixed.

Geo. H. Moore, sworn—Resides in Louisville, KY, was born there and resided there for the last six years. Am son of Geo. J. Moore, of Louisville; there is only one Geo. J. Moore there of my knowledge. Knew the negro, Daniel, in Louisville, KY. Knew him first when I was very small—have known him within the last two years—don't know his master's name, think it was Fraser. Knew him at my father's about four months before he left—my father purchased him of Fraser in 1850—he ran away in August 1850. My father had no other servant of the name of Daniel. I was present when he was bargained for. Bargain was made in Louisville. I did not know at the time of his escape but knew of it shortly after. I have no doubt of his being the person. I shall be seventeen the 10th of next January.

Cross Examined.—I have never seen the record made up

in the county court of Jefferson county, KY. I do not know that he is the person described in that record. My father owns no other slaves but this one. I was at Louisville at the time of the alleged escape. Was at home at the time. Heard the bargain between my father and Fraser at Louisville, about five or six months before Daniel left. My father bought him for $700; do not know how it was to be paid of if there was an agreement for time. Have no knowledge of the payment of the money—thinks he, Daniel, ran on the river, am not sure—Daniel was not present at the bargain. Don't know where he was. Didn't hear any description given as part of the bargain. Father was well acquainted with Daniel. Didn't know whether he resided in or near Louisville. Mr. Rust told me the man's name was Fraser owned the slave. Daniel was cook part of the time, part a steward on a Steamboat—while not on the boat he was at my father's house. Father did not own the Steamboat. Have seen him at the house several times. He was cook on the *Anna Lennington*, when he escaped. He was hired out—don't know for how long. His name is Daniel—don't know his surname—have heard him called Daniel. Can't tell the exact number of times I have seen him at my father's. He is alleged to have escaped about the 25th August, 1850, from the boat. She was a regular boat to Cincinnati. He went there as steward of the boat.

Here the defense claimed that the act of taking the slave to a free state enfranchised him, but his Honor, the Commissioner, held that the slave was not taken into a free state by his master—but that even if he had, that act could not have the effect to enfranchise him, as any master has a right to take his slave through or into a free state.

Here the defense proposed to introduce testimony to destroy the identity, by proving that the prisoner had been longer in a free state than since the time of the alleged escaped, but after waiting a considerable time and the defense not producing any witnesses, the Commissioner decided that the proof was sufficient to warrant his commitment.

The Commissioner then made and signed the certificate required by the act of Congress, authorizing the agent of the claimant to take the slave back to his master.

The fugitive was then taken to jail; without disturbance or any effort at hindrance.

Commissioner Smith, on announcing his decision, remarked that whatever we might in this section think of slavery itself, the law must be executed—that the slave Daniel must be sent back to his master, it had been shown that he was purchased for $700, and he didn't know what others might do, for the purpose of securing his freedom, but he would contribute $25.

John L. Talcott, Esq., announced to the colored people that the Agent had no authority to make any arrangement for the sale of the slave but would immediately telegraph to Louisville to his owner; and that he would not be removed until a reply was received.

The Commissioner remarked to the colored people, in pretty emphatic terms, that the law would be executed at all hazards and that any attempt at rescue would be met in a summary manner.

Thus ended the first Fugitive Slave case in Buffalo.—The law was allowed to take its course, regularly and speedily, even in the face of the strongest prejudices against slavery. All good citizens acquiesced—but few noisy, brawling men attempted to create disturbance, in which they signally [i.e., conspicuously] failed.

Great credit is due to the Sheriff—the Commissioner, the Deputy Marshal and his assistants, and to Mayor Wadsworth, for the firmness and energy, with which they discharged an unpleasant duty. As the Courier remarks, the conduct of Mayor Wadsworth, was quiet but decided throughout. He walked by the door of the carriage containing the fugitive, from the Commissioner's office to the Court House, and although several efforts were made by some of the crowd who surrounded the carriage to open the door, he kept his position firmly and discharged his duty faithfully. His course in the whole matter contrasted strongly with some few of whom better things were expected, as law-abiding citizens, of whom we may take occasion to speak hereafter.

Buffalo Commercial Advertiser
August 19, 1851

CASE OF MR. RUST.

Mr. Rust came before the Police Court about five o'clock last evening, pleaded guilty to the charge of Assault and Battery, and was fined $50—amply sufficient as such matters go—but not enough, of course, to satisfy the abolitionists or their organs.

We understand that Mr. Rust has a writ served on him for "private damages" to the slave Daniel. If a verdict is obtained, we suppose the sum awarded will go to the master—he being in law the one pecuniarily "damaged" by the transaction . . .

Buffalo Morning Express
August 30, 1851

The colored man Daniel was arrested with a billet of wood, and by the aid of a summary and exparte proceedings under the 10th section of the slave law and the equally summary and illegal ruling of the Commissioner—laid by the heels and incarcerated in a dungeon cell of our jail. With an order in the hands of the Marshal to take him to Kentucky which also adjudged that he is the slave of one Mr. Moore of Louisville, the prospects of Daniel are rather gloomy. Rust, the agent of Moore and who cut such a striking figure in the process of arresting and broiling Daniel on the stove preparatory to bringing him before the officer, was also in durance held to $1,000 bail in an action for assault and battery, in which action Daniel is plaintiff. The compromisers having got rather sick of the bludgeon process of executing laws in Buffalo now resort to the "Suaviter in modo" [smoothly in method] and Mr. Moore the claimant of Daniel appears and goes into jail, after a cosy interview with Daniel, to sign a release of the civil action against Rust for the assault. By what means Daniel was induced to release his action against Rust for being beaten and broiled, we will not now state, suffice it to say, he was in durance vile and supposed that he was subjected to the will and mercy of Moore and that he was to be taken back to Kentucky as his slave. It is not to be wondered at that he should do his master's bidding! It is said, we don't know whether it be true, that Moore gave Daniel $20 for the release—it may be so, as it would be a safe investment, as the $20 would come back naturally when they got back to Kentucky! This is the first piece of sleight of hand performed in this drama, and the actors will not have to live long, to become ashamed of this imposition upon an imprisoned and ignorant negro.

We anticipated that the customary lie to the effect that the man desires to go into slavery would be forthcoming in due time. We have been waiting for it for several days, and here it is. We put it on record:

To the Colored Population of Buffalo:

I thank you for what you have tried to do for me. You meant it for good but it is of no use. We colored people of Kentucky are about as well off as you are. I am going back—I had rather go than stay here. I hope you will not interfere with my going. My master, Mr. Moore, has always treated me well; I feel that I did wrong in running away—he bought me at my urgent request; he placed confidence in me, and I do not feel that I ought to deceive him. If he had treated me ill I should feel differently about it. He never did. I was advised to run away and come to a free State, or I should not have done so; the advice was bad, though I reckon it was not so meant. We are about as well off in Kentucky as you are here, and some of us better. I shall advise the Kentucky boys, when I get home, to stay where they are. We have plenty to eat and to wear and are not so badly worked—this every body knows who has been in Kentucky.

Again, my colored brethren, I thank you for your kind sympathies, and to my white Abolition brethren in Buffalo, I wish you the same, but I do not want you to do any more for me.

Daniel Davis, his X mark

August 28, 1851

New York Daily Tribune
September 2, 1851

DANIEL IN THE DEN AND OUT.

It was [British poet and humanist] Tom Hood, if we mistake not, who gave us all a hearty laugh some ten years since by two contemporary letters from a boy at school to his family, the first being the one written under the dictation and eye of the master; the second being the boy's own, written "unbeknown" to the master and dispatched on the sly. The contrast in the drift, tone, substance and diction of the two letters was very decided.

The *Express* and several lower-law co-laborers have been taken in by a letter purporting to be from Daniel, the alleged fugitive from Slavery in prison at Buffalo, which the least sprinkling of gumption would have told them was the Master's letter and not the Boy's Own. In this precious epistle, the knocked-down and head-broken fugitive is made to discourse Silvery Grey music [that is, in flowery eloquence not common to illiterate slaves].

The *Express*, which has a very poor idea of Negro capacity in general, was greatly taken with this effusion, commenting on it as follows:

> This man Daniel, is evidently a person gifted with considerable more common sense and shrewdness than we are accustomed to look for among people of his class and color. In this letter of his he has manifested a keen power of penetration, which distinguishes him as an excellent judge of character. He has discrimination too, and a remarkable readiness in divining men's motives, with a particular aptitude of analysis in cases where hypocrisy and false pretenses are mixed up with a lying philanthropy and the schemes of the demagogue.
>
> This is the character of the man Daniel, as we infer from the sensible letter he has left as an invaluable legacy to the colored population of Buffalo. And being so intelligent and shrewd a person, what he writes, we repeat, is entitled to a profounder consideration than is commonly conceded to ordinary productions of negro literature.

Well: two days after the appearance of this letter, and before the *Express* had done singing its praises, Judge Conkling pronounced a decision which set this new star in the Literary firmament at liberty. No obstacle existed to his following his own inclination, whichever way it might head him. Of course, you suppose that he struck a bee-line for that patriarchal region whence he "did wrong in running away," where he was "always treated well," and where he would "advise the Kentucky boys to stay where they are," having "plenty to eat and to wear, and are not badly worked." Ah, my green friend! you should have read the Boy's Own letter! See "his X mark:"

DANIEL, THE FUGITIVE, AT LIBERTY

Buffalo, Aug. 31, 1851. The fugitive Daniel has been declared free by Judge Conklin, and has gone to Canada.

We are afraid there will be no more eulogiums on his "common sense and shrewdness," "keen power of penetration," &c., in the columns of the *Express!* "Negro Literature" is likely to be below par in that latitude for some time to come, even though the author is so intelligent and shrewd a person as Mr. Daniel Davis. This is a deceitful, changeable world.

The Abduction of a Free Black Man

Solomon Northup

> Solomon Northup's *Twelve Years a Slave* (1853) was among
> the most widely read slave narratives; its popularity as an anti-
> slavery tale was second only to that of Harriet Beecher
> Stowe's *Uncle Tom's Cabin.* His story was made all the more
> remarkable for the fact that Northup, a citizen of Saratoga,
> New York, was freeborn. Northup was an educated man earn-
> ing a productive living as carpenter, inventor, and musician.
> He had a wife and three children. But in 1841, Northup was
> abducted by tricksters who then turned him over to the ruth-
> less slave trader James H. Burch in Washington, D.C. As the
> title of his memoir indicates, Northup spent a dozen years toil-
> ing on cotton plantations in the Louisiana bayous for various
> masters. In 1853, Northup met a Canadian carpenter named
> Samuel Bass to whom he confided his story of kidnapping and
> enslavement. With Bass's help Northup was able to send a let-
> ter to his family in New York. Henry Northup, the grandson of
> the man who had originally freed Solomon's family, secured
> authorization from the New York governor and traveled to
> Louisiana to obtain Solomon's lawful freedom.
>
> In the following selection, Northup recounts his fateful
> encounter with two men who tell him they represent a circus
> eager to pay him good wages as a fiddler. Lured to the nation's
> capital, Northup is drugged and awakens to find himself in
> chains, his status as a free man wrested away from him.

Solomon Northup, *Twelve Years a Slave. Narrative of Solomon Northup, a Citizen of New-York, Kidnapped in Washington City in 1841, and Rescued in 1853, from a Cotton Plantation Near the Red River, in Louisiana.* Auburn: Derby and Miller, 1853.

One morning, towards the latter part of the month of March, 1841, having at that time no particular business to engage my attention, I was walking about the village of Saratoga Springs, thinking to myself where I might obtain some present employment until the busy season should arrive. Anne, as was her usual custom, had gone over to Sandy Hill, a distance of some twenty miles, to take charge of the culinary department at Sherrill's Coffee House during the session of the court. Elizabeth, I think, had accompanied her. Margaret and Alonzo were with their aunt at Saratoga.

On the corner of Congress street and Broadway, near the tavern, then, and for aught I know to the contrary, still kept by Mr. Moon, I was met by two gentlemen of respectable appearance, both of whom were entirely unknown to me. I have the impression that they were introduced to me by some one of my acquaintances, but who, I have in vain endeavored to recall, with the remark that I was an expert player on the violin.

A Tempting Job Offer

At any rate, they immediately entered into conversation on that subject, making numerous inquiries touching my proficiency in that respect. My responses being to all appearances satisfactory, they proposed to engage my services for a short period, stating, at the same time, I was just such a person as their business required. Their names, as they afterwards gave them to me, were Merrill Brown and Abram Hamilton, though whether these were their true appellations, I have strong reasons to doubt. The former was a man apparently forty years of age, somewhat short and thick-set, with a countenance indicating shrewdness and intelligence. He wore a black frock coat and black hat and said he resided either at Rochester or at Syracuse. The latter was a young man of fair complexion and light eyes and, I should judge, had not passed the age of twenty-five. He was tall and slender, dressed in a snuff-colored coat, with glossy hat, and vest of elegant pattern. His whole apparel was in the extreme of fashion. His appearance was somewhat effeminate but prepossessing, and there was about him an easy air that showed he had mingled with the world. They were connected, as they informed me, with a circus company then in the city of Washington; that they were on their way thither to rejoin it, having left it for a short time to make an excursion northward, for the purpose of seeing the country, and were paying their expenses by an occasional exhibition. They also remarked that they had found much difficulty in procuring music for their entertainments, and that if I would accompany them as far as New York, they would give me one dollar for each day's services and three dollars in addition for every night I played at their performances, besides sufficient to pay the expenses of my return from New York to Saratoga.

I at once accepted the tempting offer, both for the reward it promised and from a desire to visit the metropolis. They were anxious to leave immediately. Thinking my absence would be brief, I did not deem it necessary to write to Anne whither I had gone; in fact supposing that my return, perhaps, would be as soon as hers. So taking a change of linen and my violin, I was ready to depart. The carriage was brought round—a covered one, drawn by a pair of noble bays, altogether forming an elegant establishment. Their baggage, consisting of three large trunks, was fastened on the rack, and mounting to the driver's seat, while they took their places in the rear, I drove away from Saratoga on the road to Albany, elated with my new position and happy as I had ever been on any day, in all my life.

A Fateful Journey Begins

We passed through Ballston, and striking the ridge road, as it is called, if my memory correctly serves me, followed it direct to Albany. We reached that city before dark, and stopped at a hotel southward from the Museum.

This night I had an opportunity of witnessing one of their performances—the only one during the whole period I was with them. Hamilton was stationed at the door; I formed the orchestra, while Brown provided the entertainment. It consisted in throwing balls, dancing on the rope, frying pancakes in a hat, causing invisible pigs to squeal, and other like feats of ventriloquism and legerdemain. The audience was extraordinarily sparse and not of the selectest character at that, and Hamilton's report of the proceeds presented but a "beggarly account of empty boxes."

Early next morning we renewed our journey. The burden of their conversation now was the expression of an anxiety to reach the circus without delay. They hurried forward without again stopping to exhibit, and in due course of time, we reached New York, taking lodgings at a house on the west side of the city, in a street running from Broadway to the river. I supposed my journey was at an end and expected in a day or two at least to return to my friends and family at Saratoga. Brown and Hamilton, however, began to importune me to continue with them to Washington. They alleged that immediately on their arrival, now that the summer season was approaching, the circus would set out for the north. They promised me a situation and high wages if I would accompany them. Largely did they expatiate on the advantages that would result to me, and such were the flattering representations they made, that I finally concluded to accept the offer.

Proof of Freedom

The next morning they suggested that, inasmuch as we were about entering a slave state, it would be well, before leaving New York, to procure free papers. The idea struck me as a prudent one, though I think it would scarcely have occurred to me had they not proposed it. We proceeded at once to what I understood to be the Custom House. They made oath to certain facts showing I was a free man. A paper was drawn up and handed us, with the direction to take it to the clerk's office. We did so, and the clerk having added something to it, for which he was paid six shillings, we returned again to the Custom House. Some further formalities were gone through with before it was completed, when, paying the officer two dollars, I placed the papers in my pocket, and started with my two friends to our hotel. I thought at the time, I must confess, that the papers were scarcely worth the cost of obtaining them—the apprehension of danger to my personal safety never having suggested itself to me in the remotest manner. The clerk, to whom we were directed, I remember, made a memorandum in a large book, which, I presume, is in the office yet. A reference to the entries during the latter part of March or first of April, 1841, I have no doubt will satisfy the incredulous, at least so far as this particular transaction is concerned.

With the evidence of freedom in my profession, the next day after our arrival in New York, we crossed the ferry to Jersey City and took the road to Philadelphia. Here we remained one night, continuing our journey towards Baltimore early in the morning. In due time, we arrived in the latter city, and stopped at a hotel near the railroad depot, either kept by a Mr. Rathbone or known as the Rathbone House. All the way from New York, their anxiety to reach the circus seemed to grow more and more intense. We left the carriage at Baltimore and, entering the cars, proceeded to Washington, at which place we arrived just at nightfall, the evening previous to the funeral of General [William Henry] Harrison [the former president who died on April 4, 1841], and stopped at Gadsby's Hotel, on Pennsylvania Avenue.

Trust Misplaced

After supper, they called me to their apartments and paid me forty-three dollars, a sum greater than my wages amounted to, which act of generosity was in consequence, they said, of their not having exhibited as often as they had given me to anticipate during our trip from Saratoga. They moreover informed me that it had been the intention of the circus company to leave Washington the next morning, but that on account of the funeral, they had concluded to remain another day. They were then, as they had been from the time of our first meeting, extremely kind. No opportunity was omitted of addressing me in the language of approbation; while, on the other hand, I was certainly much prepossessed in their favor. I gave them my confidence without reserve and would freely have trusted them to almost any extent. Their constant conversation and manner towards me—their foresight in suggesting the idea of free papers and a hundred other little acts unnecessary to be repeated—all indicated that they were friends indeed, sincerely solicitous for my welfare. I know not but they were. I know not but they were innocent of the great wickedness of which I now believe them guilty. Whether they were accessory to my misfortunes—subtle and inhuman monsters in the shape of men—designedly luring me away from home and family, and liberty, for the sake of gold—those who read these pages will have the same means of determining as myself. If they were innocent, my sudden disappearance must have been unaccountable indeed; but revolving in my mind all the attending circumstances, I never yet could indulge towards them so charitable a supposition.

After receiving the money from them, of which they appeared to have an abundance, they advised me not to go into the streets that night, inasmuch as I was unacquainted with the customs of the city. Promising to remember their advice, I left them together and soon after was shown by a colored servant to a sleeping room in the back part of the hotel on the ground floor. I laid down to rest, thinking of home and wife, and children, and the long distance that stretched between us, until I fell asleep. But no good angel of pity came to my bedside, bidding me to fly—no voice of mercy forewarned me in my dreams of the trials that were just at hand.

The next day there was a great pageant in Washington. The roar of cannon and the tolling of bells filled the air, while many houses were shrouded with crape, and the streets were black with people. As the day advanced, the procession made its appearance, coming slowly through the Avenue, carriage after carriage, in long succession, while thousands upon thousands followed on foot—all moving to the sound of melancholy music. They were bearing the dead body of Harrison to the grave.

From early in the morning, I was constantly in the company of Hamilton and Brown. They were the only persons I knew in Washington. We stood together as the funeral pomp passed by. I remember distinctly how the window glass would break and rattle to the ground, after each report of the cannon they were firing in the burial ground. We went to the Capitol and walked a long time about the grounds. In the afternoon, they strolled towards the President's House, all the time keeping me near to them and pointing out various places of interest. As yet, I had seen nothing of the circus. In fact, I had thought of it but little, if at all, amidst the excitement of the day.

Poison and Betrayal

My friends, several times during the afternoon, entered drinking saloons and called for liquor. They were by no means in the habit, however, so far as I knew them, of indulging to excess. On these occasions, after serving themselves, they would pour out a glass and hand it to me. I did not become intoxicated, as may be inferred from what subsequently occurred. Towards evening, and soon after partaking of one of these potations, I began to experience most unpleasant sensations. I felt extremely ill. My head commenced aching—a dull, heavy pain, inexpressibly disagreeable. At the supper table, I was without appetite; the sight and flavor of food was nauseous. About dark the same servant conducted me to the room I had occupied the previous night. Brown and Hamilton advised me to retire, commiserating me kindly, and expressing hopes that I would be better in the morning. Divesting myself of coat and boots merely, I threw myself upon the bed. It was impossible to sleep. The pain in my head continued to increase until it became almost unbearable. In a short time I became thirsty. My lips were parched. I could think of nothing but water—of lakes and flowing rivers, of brooks where I had stopped to drink, and of the dripping bucket, rising with its cool and overflowing nectar, from the bottom of the well. Towards midnight, as near as I could judge, I arose, unable longer to bear such intensity of thirst. I was a stranger in the house, and knew nothing of its apartments. There was no one up, as I could observe. Groping about at random, I knew not where, I found the way at last to a kitchen in the basement. Two or three colored servants were moving through it, one of whom, a woman, gave me two glasses of water. It afforded momentary relief, but by the time I had reached my room again, the same burning desire of drink, the some tormenting thirst, had again returned. It was even more torturing than before, as was also the wild pain in my head, if such a thing could be. I was in sore distress—in most excruciating agony! I seemed to stand on the brink of madness! The memory of that night of horrible suffering will follow me to the grave.

In the course of an hour or more after my return from the kitchen, I was conscious of some one entering my room. There seemed to be several—a mingling of various voices—but how many or who they were, I cannot tell. Whether Brown and Hamilton were among them is a mere matter of conjecture. I only remember, with any degree of distinctness, that I was told it was necessary to go to a physician and procure medicine, and that pulling on my boots, without coat or hat, I followed them through a long passage-way or alley into the open street. It ran out at right angles from Pennsylvania Avenue. On the opposite side there was a light burning in a window. My impression is there were then three persons with me, but it is altogether indefinite and vague, and like the memory of a painful dream. Going towards the light, which I imagined proceeded from a physician's office, and which seemed to recede as I advanced, is the last glimmering recollection I can now recall. From that moment I was insensible. How long I remained in that condition—whether only that night, or many days and nights—I do not know; but when consciousness returned, I found myself alone, in utter darkness, and in chains.

A Free Man in Captivity

The pain in my head had subsided in a measure, but I was very faint and weak. I was sitting upon a low bench made of rough boards and without coat or hat. I was hand-cuffed. Around my ankles also were a pair of heavy fetters. One end of a chain was fastened to a large ring in the floor, the other to the fetters on my ankles. I tried in vain to stand upon my feet. Walking from such a painful trance, it was some time before I could collect my thoughts. Where was I? What was the meaning of these chains? Where were Brown and Hamilton? What had I done to deserve imprisonment in such a dungeon? I could not comprehend. There was a blank of some indefinite period preceding my awakening in that lonely place, the events of which the utmost stretch of memory was unable to recall. I listened intently for some sign or sound of life, but nothing broke the oppressive silence save the clinking of my chains whenever I chanced to move. I spoke aloud, but the sound of my voice startled me. I felt of my pockets, so far as the fetters would allow—far enough, indeed, to ascertain that I had not only been robbed of liberty, but that my money and free papers were also gone! Then did the idea begin to break upon my mind, at first dim and confused, that I had been kidnapped. But that I thought was incredible. There must have been some misapprehension—some unfortunate mistake. It could not be that a free citizen of New York, who had wronged no man, nor violated any law, should be dealt with thus inhumanly. The more I contemplated my situation, however, the more I became confirmed in my suspicions. It was a desolate thought, indeed. I felt there was no trust or mercy in unfeeling man; and commending myself to the God of the oppressed, bowed my head upon my fettered hands and wept most bitterly.

Chronology

1619

Twenty Africans are deposited at Jamestown, Virginia, by a Dutch frigate; whether their legal status was that of slaves or servants remains unclear.

1641

Massachusetts is the first American colony to recognize slavery officially in its laws.

1671

Maryland's legislature enacts a law holding that conversion to Christianity does not alter one's slave status.

1672

Virginia passes a law rewarding the killing of "Maroons"— runaway slaves who maintain a nomadic existence on the western frontier; between 1672 and 1864 dozens of Maroon communities are formed in the forests and swamps of South Carolina, Florida, Virginia, and other colonies and states.

1688

Quakers in Germantown, Pennsylvania, denounce slavery in America's first recorded formal protest against the institution.

1723

Virginia forbids owners to free (manumit) their slaves by law.

1739

Forty-four black slaves and thirty white colonists are killed in the Stono slave rebellion near Charleston, South Carolina.

1775–1783
The British royal governor of Virginia, Lord Dunmore, issues a proclamation in November 1775 declaring those slaves free who join "his Majesty's troops." During the Revolutionary War an estimated fifty thousand slaves escape to join the British.

1776
Thomas Jefferson drafts the Declaration of Independence; the document is adopted by the Continental Congress after passages condemning the slave trade are removed.

1777
Vermont forbids slavery in its founding state constitution.

1780
Pennsylvania passes a law to gradually abolish slavery; similar laws are passed by Rhode Island and Connecticut in 1784, New York in 1799, and New Jersey in 1804.

1782
Virginia passes a law permitting the private manumission of slaves at the owner's discretion.

1787
Congress passes the Northwest Ordinance, banning slavery in the western territory north of the Ohio River acquired from England in the Revolutionary War.

1788
The Constitution, which indirectly sanctions slavery and forbids Congress from abolishing the slave trade for twenty more years, is ratified by the states.

1793
Congress passes the Fugitive Slave Law, providing for the return of slaves who have escaped across state boundaries;

Eli Whitney invents the cotton gin, which greatly increases the demand for slaves.

1800
Gabriel Prosser is captured and hanged after his planned slave rebellion in Virginia is betrayed and thwarted.

1808
Congress forbids the importation of slaves into the United States.

1816
The American Colonization Society, which seeks to return slaves and free blacks to Africa, is founded.

1820
Congress passes the Missouri Compromise, admitting Missouri as a slave state and Maine as a free state; it also draws a line (at 36°30' north latitude) dividing the remaining Louisiana Territory (purchased from France in 1803) into slave and free regions.

1822
Denmark Vesey, a free black, is executed after his five-year effort to organize a slave rebellion in Charleston, South Carolina, is betrayed by an informant.

1831
William Lloyd Garrison publishes the first issue of the *Liberator*, his abolitionist newspaper, in January; in August, Nat Turner leads a slave revolt in Virginia that results in the deaths of sixty whites and more than two hundred blacks, including Turner, who is captured and executed; southern states pass new laws to prevent future rebellions.

1833

The American Anti-Slavery Society is founded; slavery is abolished in the British Empire.

1836–1844

Congress imposes a gag rule automatically tabling all anti-slavery petitions and preventing discussion of the issue; it is repealed after eight years at the urging of former president John Quincy Adams.

1838

Frederick Douglass escapes from slavery to New York City, where he establishes himself as a leading black abolitionist.

1840

The abolitionist movement splits over whether to engage in political activity; the Liberty Party is founded and fields a presidential candidate.

1845

Texas is admitted to the Union as a slave state.

1846–1849

U.S. victory in the Mexican War raises the question of whether America's newly acquired territories should permit slavery; Congressman David Wilmot introduces but fails to pass the Wilmot Proviso in 1846 banning slavery in all territory acquired from Mexico.

1849

Harriet Tubman escapes from slavery in Maryland to freedom in Philadelphia; she will return to the South nineteen times to help slaves escape via the Underground Railroad.

1850

Congress passes the Compromise of 1850; California is admitted as a free state, New Mexico and Utah are admitted as territories with the power to decide the issue on their own ("popular sovereignty"), the slave trade is abolished in Washington, D.C., and a tougher Fugitive Slave Act is passed penalizing people who interfere with the capture and return of escaped slaves.

1852

Harriet Beecher Stowe's novel *Uncle Tom's Cabin* is published.

1854

Congress passes the Kansas-Nebraska Act, organizing those territories under the principle of popular sovereignty; the law voids the 1820 Missouri Compromise by potentially permitting slavery north of the 36°30' dividing line; negative reaction to the Kansas-Nebraska Act leads to the creation of the Republican Party.

1855–1858

The Kansas territory becomes a political and military battleground over the expansion of slavery in the area.

1857

The U.S. Supreme Court in *Dred Scott v. Sandford* abrogates the Missouri Compromise line dividing slave and free territory and declares that blacks "had no rights the white man was bound to respect."

1859

John Brown leads an unsuccessful raid on the federal armory in Harpers Ferry, Virginia, hoping to start a general slave revolt.

1860

Abraham Lincoln is elected president on a platform of restricting slavery in the territories; South Carolina secedes from the Union.

1861–1865
The Civil War follows the secession of the Southern states amid concerns over the preservation of slavery; thousands of slaves escape during the conflict, are declared "contraband of war," and serve the Union war effort; an estimated 250,000 African Americans, some of whom were slaves, serve as soldiers.

1863
President Lincoln's Emancipation Proclamation, announced in September 1862, takes effect on January 1; it frees slaves held in the Confederate states.

1865
The Thirteenth Amendment to the Constitution, abolishing slavery throughout the United States, is ratified.

For Further Research

Historical Studies

Herbert Aptheker, *Abolitionism: A Revolutionary Movement.* Boston: G.K. Hall/Twayne, 1989.

R.J.M. Blackett, *Building an Antislavery Wall.* Baton Rouge: Louisiana State University Press, 1983.

William Breyfogle, *Make Free: The Story of the Underground Railroad.* Philadelphia: J.B. Lippincott, 1958.

Henrietta Buckmaster, *Flight to Freedom: The Story of the Underground Railroad.* New York: Dell, 1972.

Eric Foner, *Free Soil, Free Labor, Free Men.* New York: Oxford University Press, 1970.

John Hope Franklin, *From Slavery to Freedom.* New York: Alfred A. Knopf, 1979.

V.P. Franklin, *Black Self-Determination: A Cultural History of African American Resistance.* Brooklyn, NY: Lawrence Hill, 1992.

George M. Fredrickson, *The Arrogance of Race: Historical Perspectives on Slavery, Racism, and Social Inequality.* Middletown, CT: Wesleyan University Press, 1988.

Larry Gara, *The Liberty Line: The Legend of the Underground Railroad.* Lexington: University of Kentucky Press, 1961.

Henry Louis Gates, ed., *The Classic Slave Narratives.* New York: Mentor, 1987.

Stanley Harrold, *The Abolitionists and the South, 1831–1861.* Lexington: University Press of Kentucky, 1995.

Daniel G. Hill, *The Freedom Seekers: Blacks in Early Canada.* Agincourt: Book Society of Canada, 1981.

Michael Holt, *The Political Crisis of the 1850s.* New York: Wiley, 1978.

James Oliver Horton, *Free People of Color: Inside the African American Community.* Washington, DC: Smithsonian Institution Press, 1993.

Charles Johnson, Patricia Smith, and the WGBH Series Research Team, *Africans in America: America's Journey Through Slavery.* San Diego: Harvest/Harcourt Brace, 1998.

Jonathan Katz, *Resistance at Christiana: The Fugitive Slave Rebellion, Christiana, Pennsylvania, September 11, 1851.* New York: Thomas Y. Crowell, 1974.

Aileen Kraditor, *Means and Ends in American Abolitionism.* New York: Ivan Dee, 1989.

Dan Lacy, *The Abolitionists.* New York: McGraw-Hill, 1978.

Stephen R. Lilley, *Fighters Against American Slavery.* San Diego: Lucent, 1998.

Henry Mayer, *All on Fire: William Lloyd Garrison and the Abolition of Slavery.* New York: St. Martin's, 1998.

James M. McPherson, *The Struggle for Equality: Abolitionists and the Negro in the Civil War and Reconstruction.* Princeton, NJ: Princeton University Press, 1964.

Arch Merrill, *The Underground, Freedom's Road.* New York: American Book-Stratford Press, 1963.

Edmund Morgan, *American Slavery, American Freedom.* New York: Norton, 1975.

Charles H. Nicholas, *Many Thousands Gone: The Ex-Slaves' Accounts of Their Bondage and Freedom.* Leiden, Netherlands: Brill, 1963.

Jane H. Pease and William H. Pease, *They Who Would Be Free: Blacks' Search for Freedom, 1830–1861.* New York: Atheneum, 1974.

Benjamin Quarles, *Black Abolitionists.* New York: Oxford University Press, 1969.

Shirley Samuels, ed., *The Culture of Sentiment: Race, Gender, and Sentimentality in Nineteenth-Century America.* New York: Oxford University Press, 1992.

Wilbur H. Siebert, *The Underground Railroad: From Slavery to Freedom.* New York: Macmillan, 1898.

Sterling Stuckey, *Slave Culture.* New York: Oxford University Press, 1987.

Robin W. Winks, *The Blacks in Canada: A History.* New Haven, CT: Yale University Press, 1971.

Primary Sources

Ray Allen Billington, ed., *A Free Negro in the Slave Era: The Journal of Charlotte L. Forten.* New York: Collier, 1961.

Charles L. Blockson, *The Underground Railroad: Dramatic First-Hand Accounts of Daring Escapes to Freedom.* New York: Berkley, 1987.

Benjamin Drew, *A North-Side View of Slavery. The Refugee; or The Narratives of Fugitive Slaves in Canada Related by Themselves.* Boston: J.P. Jewett, 1856.

Deirdre Mullane, ed., *Crossing the Danger Water: Three Hundred Years of African American Writing.* New York: Anchor/Bantam Doubleday/Dell, 1993.

Richard Newman, Patrick Rael, and Philip Lapsansky, eds., *Pamphlets of Protest: An Anthology of Early African American Protest Literature, 1790–1860.* New York: Routledge, 2001.

C. Peter Ripley et al., eds., *The Black Abolitionist Papers: The British Isles, 1830–1865.* Chapel Hill: University of North Carolina Press, 1985.

William Still, *Underground Railroad Records.* Philadelphia: W. Still, 1872.

Websites

American Memory, www.memory.loc.gov. The Library of Congress's American Memory collection is an invaluable electronic archive of primary documents significant for the study of American history, politics, and culture. American Memory provides access to more than 7 million digital items, including the African American Pamphlet Collection, a vast archival resource of original documents concerning slavery, abolition, and the struggle for freedom.

Documenting the American South, www.metalab.unc.edu. Documenting the American South offers a wealth of primary documents relevant to the American southern experience from colonial times to the early twentieth century. It is an especially good source for slave narratives and other rare first-person narratives (memoirs, diaries, letters, and travel writing).

Douglass Archives of American Public Address, www. pubweb.northwestern.edu. Named for Frederick Douglass, this electronic archive published by Northwestern University contains speeches from 1645 through the present dealing with important social, political, and historical issues in U.S. history.

Electronic Oberlin Group: Oberlin Through History, www. oberlin.edu/~EOG. Oberlin College's archives include an online collection of important primary materials on Oberlin and Ohio before, during, and after the Civil War. Documents on the abolitionist movement, the Underground Railroad, and the postwar quest for equal rights can be found here.

Index

abolitionist movement. *See* antislavery movement
Adams, James, 43
advertisements, 42
  for capture of abolitionists, 146, 156
  for capture of runaway slaves, 113, 130
African Americans, free, 56, 125, 161
  abduction of, 200, 201–208
  abolitionists among, 18
  communities and, 15
  discrimination against, 16, 25
    harassment and, 57, 99–100
    need to carry proof of freedom and, 203–204
    restrictive laws concerning travel and, 101
  Fugitive Slave Act a problem for, 171
  portrayed as overworked, by slaveholders, 190
agriculture, 13–15, 54
Alatamah River, 90
American Anti-Slavery Society, 17, 83, 116, 129
antislavery materials, 19, 125–27
  possession of, was illegal, 122
antislavery movement, 14, 24, 68, 94, 108
  accused of interfering in South, 171, 187–88
  in Britain, 83
  in Canada, 43
  denunciation of 1850 Fugitive Slave Act by, 172
  increased support for, after 1850 Fugitive Slave Act, 170
  protest against arrest of Anthony Burns and, 114–18
  tensions between black and white abolitionists in, 16–18
  violence and, 27–28
  see also Underground Railroad; vigilance committees
Anti-Slavery Sewing Society, 145
Arkansas, 101
Ashtabula County, Ohio, 21
Auld, Hugh, 33–35
Auld, Sophia, 29
Auld, Thomas, 32, 33

Bailey, Frederick, 29
Baltimore, Maryland, 16, 32, 35, 204
Bass, Samuel, 200
Beard, William, 147
Beloved (Morrison), 119
Big Dipper, 55, 59
Billington, Ray Allen, 114
Black Seminoles, 13
Blockson, Charles L., 12
Bogguess family, 38–39
Booth, Sherman, 170
Boston, 16, 23, 73, 129
  protests in, over recapture of Anthony Burns, 114–18
Boston Vigilance Committee (antislavery group), 115
Bradford, Sarah H., 128
Brown, Henry "Box," 30, 59, 60, 171
Brown, John, 18, 24
Brown, William Wells, 25, 94, 106, 107, 171
  first-person escape narrative written by, 13, 19–20
  as Underground Railroad conductor, 12, 134
Browning, Elizabeth Barrett, 116
Buffalo, New York, 51, 107, 190, 191, 195
Buffalo Commercial Advertiser, 190
Buffalo Morning Express, 190
Burns, Anthony (fugitive slave), 23, 114–18
Bushnell, Simeon, 170
Bustill, Joseph C., 18, 141

Cable, Jonathan, 144, 145
Calhoun, John C., 182, 184, 188
California, 23, 170, 180
Canada, 11, 38, 135, 147, 191
  Anti-Slavery Society of, 43
  as destination for runaway slaves, 45, 51–52, 127, 145, 171–72
  focus of dreams and, 112, 123–24
  increased appeal of
    after 1850 Fugitive Slave Act, 43
    after War of 1812, 16
  joy on reaching, 155
  emigration of free blacks to, 83
  narratives of former slaves compiled

in, 20
opportunities in "Canada West" and,
 21
Caribbean, 11, 14, 106
Cary, Mary Ann Shadd, 21, 22
Chester, Thomas K., 156
Child, Lydia Maria, 68
children, 138, 140, 142, 147, 159
 bribed by slaveholder to betray mother,
 72–73
 killed by mother to prevent return to
 slavery, 119–21
 watched from mother's hiding place,
 70–71, 80, 81
Christiana, Pennsylvania, 22
Cincinnati, 138, 142, 147, 161
Circuit Courts, U.S., 127, 157, 172–73
Civil War, 11, 24, 29, 68
Cleveland, Ohio, 49–51
Coffin, Catherine, 146, 147
Coffin, Levi, 13, 119, 135, 146–47, 153
 as prominent Quaker, 12, 157
 as Underground Railroad conductor,
 106, 134, 148
colonization, 16–17, 21
Compromise of 1850, 23, 170, 171, 180
Confederate States of America (CSA),
 24
Congress, U.S., 19, 171, 180, 186
Constitution, U.S., 173–74, 185–86, 189
Craft, Ellen and William, 13, 59, 94, 171

Davis, Daniel (fugitive slave), 190, 199
 arrest of, 191
 fabricated letter of, 197–98
 trial of, 192, 193–94
 returned to owner, 195–96
Delaware, 157
democracy, 112
Detroit, 146
*Different Mirror: A History of
 Multicultural America, A* (Takaki),
 86–87
Dillingham, Richard (Quaker
 abolitionist), 160
 death of, 168
 imprisonment of, 161–63, 167
 trial of, 164–66
District Court, U.S., 176–77
District of Columbia, 178
Douglass, Frederick, 25, 29, 83, 107
 Anthony Burns case and, 115
 fugitive slave bill and, 175
 first-person escape narrative written by,
 13, 19–20
 offended by white abolitionists, 17
Dred Scott decision, 23

Drew, Benjamin, 13, 20, 43, 53

economy, 14–15
education, 41, 83, 115, 146, 156, 161
 denied to slaves, 53–54, 59, 98, 123,
 135
emancipation, 17, 134
Emancipation Proclamation, 29
England, 16, 60, 77, 97, 108
 black abolitionists fled to, 83, 171
 Craft's autobiography published in, 94
escape journeys, 36, 39–41, 79, 87–92,
 102
 by boat, 51, 64, 93
 dangers of, 78, 86, 152
 included being sent "down river,"
 147
 included death, 106
 included punishment, 95
 included risk of betrayal, 45–46, 78,
 80, 153–54
 disguise and, 96–99
 by race, 84, 90, 92
 groups of runaways and, 119, 120,
 153–54
 hardships of, 139–40, 142–43
 joy of arrival and, 66–67, 155
 need for secrecy about, 30–31, 147
 North Star as guide on, 111, 128, 140,
 165
 preparations for, 34–35, 110, 149–51
 rare opportunities for, 77
 separation of families and, 81–82
 by train, 103–104
 through wilderness, 48
Europe, 11, 15

Fairfield, John, 142–43
families, separation of, 39, 52, 94–95,
 113, 124
 desperate acts prompted by, 148–49
 through limited opportunities for
 escape, 75–76, 80–82
 through sales of family members to
 different buyers, 74, 107–109
Fillmore, Millard, 180
Florida, 13, 84, 87, 90
"Follow the Drinking Gourd" (song), 55,
 59
Fort Sumner, 24
Forten, Charlotte, 114
Franklin, Benjamin, 14
Frederick Douglass's Paper
 (newspaper), 175
freedom, 20, 36, 87, 117, 159
 could be secured by visit to free state,
 121

government hypocritical about, 118
as human right, 116
strength of longing for, 39, 87
Fugitive Aid Society, 141
Fugitive Slave Act (1850), 24, 107, 134, 190
  abolitionist reaction to, 172, 175
  Anthony Burns returned to owner under, 114
  citizens required to assist in apprehension of runaways by, 129, 170, 180
    including antislavery Northerners, 185–87, 195
  duty of law officers and, 173
  motivation of fugitive slaves to leave country intensified by, 23, 43, 94
  Northerners enraged by, 115
  payment for aiding an arrest and, 177–78
  proof of ownership and, 175, 179
  punishment of people helping fugitive slaves mandated by, 20, 176
  resistance to, 21, 22
  sectional discord exacerbated by, 171
  slaveholders' right to reclaim fugitives supported by, 174
Fugitive Slave Law (1793), 15–16, 20, 171

Garlick, Anson Kirby, 41–42
Garlick, Charles A., 38
Garner, Margaret, 119–21
Garrett, Thomas, 12, 134, 157
Garrison, William Lloyd, 17, 24, 94, 117, 165
  Anthony Burns case and, 115
  Fugitive Slave Act and, 180
Gates, G.B., 191–92
Georgia, 87, 94, 101, 104
  difficulty of escaping from, 84, 96
  racism in, 99–100
  see also Savannah, Georgia
Glover, Joshua, 22, 23
Gorsuch, Edward, 22
Green, Samuel, Jr., 122–24, 127
Green, Samuel, Sr., 122, 124–27
Grimes, Leonard, 114, 115

Harpers Ferry siege, 24
Harriet: The Moses of Her People (Bradford), 128
Harris, Benjamin, 43, 44, 51
  on escape journey with Adams, 45–50
Harrison, William Henry, 180, 204, 205
Hatfield, John, 143, 144
Haviland, Laura S., 106, 146

Hawkins, Samuel and Emeline, 158–59
Henderson, Francis, 53
Hopper, Isaac T., 14
House of Delegates, U.S., 188
House of Representatives, U.S., 172
Hunn, John, 158–59

illiteracy, 91, 94, 98
imprisonment, 108, 109, 113
  of people helping runaway slaves, 125–26, 158, 160–63, 167–68, 170
  of people teaching slaves to read, 98
  for possession of abolition pamphlets, 127
  of recaptured slaves, 116, 121, 195
Incidents in the Life of a Slave Girl (Jacobs), 68

Jacobs, Harriet, 13, 19, 68, 130
Jewett, John P., 43
Johnson, Charles, 15, 17–18
Journal of Charlotte Forten, The (Forten), 114

Kansas-Nebraska Act (1854), 23–24
Kentucky, 101, 121, 191, 193, 197
  case of slave who temporarily returned to master in, 148–51
  Ohio River a crossing point for slaves escaping from, 146
Key to Uncle Tom's Cabin, The (Stowe), 13, 157, 160

Lapsansky, Philip, 21
Liberator (antislavery newspaper), 17
Life, Including His Escape and Struggle for Liberty, of Charles A. Garlick, Born a Slave in Old Virginia, Who Secured His Freedom by Running Away from His Master's Farm in 1843 (Charles A. Garlick), 38
Lincoln, Abraham, 22, 24, 29, 134
Loguen, J.W., 18, 87
Louisiana, 200
Louisville, Kentucky, 191, 193

Maddox, M.D., 161–62
marriage, 96
Maryland, 29, 128, 157, 159, 170
Massachusetts, 14, 118, 180
McClellan, George B., 134
McDowell, James, 188
Mchenry, Jerry, 22, 23
Methodist Church, 45, 51
Methodist Episcopal Church, 183
Mexico, 11, 106
Michigan, 21, 146, 152

Midwest, 146
Mississippi, 101, 107
Missouri Compromise (1821), 23
Moore, G.H., 192, 193, 196, 197
Morrison, Toni, 119
Mott, Lucretia, 12, 134
Muse, James (slaveholder), 123

Nalle, Charles (fugitive slave), 23, 129–32
Narrative of the Adventures and Escape of Moses Roper from American Slavery (Roper), 83
Narrative of Henry "Box" Brown, Who Escaped from Slavery, (Henry "Box" Brown), 60
Narrative of the Life of Frederick Douglass: An American Slave, Written by Himself (Douglass), 29
Narrative of William W. Brown, a Fugitive Slave (William Wells Brown), 107
Nashville, Tennessee, 161, 168, 176
Nashville Daily Gazette, 166–67
Natchez, Mississippi, 107, 108
Native Americans, 13, 84
New Hampshire, 180
Newman, Richard, 21
New Orleans, 107, 108
Newport, Indiana, 135, 138, 145
New York City, 14–16, 36, 68, 73
New York Daily Tribune, 190
New York State, 21, 107
   civil disobedience in, 22–23
   destination for escaping slaves, 92, 93
Norcom, James (slaveholder), 68, 70, 75, 81, 130
   attempts to recover escaped slave Harriet Jacobs and, 71
   through bribing her children, 72–73
North Carolina, 83, 135, 182
Northerners, 170, 182, 187, 190
   bound to give up fugitives, 184–86
   denunciation of 1850 Fugitive Slave Act by, 20, 21, 129
   denunciation of Nebraska bill in, 118
   limited safety for runaway slaves among, 16
   protection of runaway slaves by, 22, 131–32
      increased involvement in, 170
      reluctance about, among some abolitionists, 134, 135, 136
North-Side View of Slavery (Drew), 13, 20, 43, 53
North Star (antislavery newspaper), 29
Northup, Solomon, 20, 200

Oakes, James, 23
Ohio, 22, 42, 153–54, 160
   home of Levi and Catherine Coffin, 147
   Underground Railroad stations in, 146
Ohio River, 12, 140, 149, 151
   accessibility of, increased by ice, 119–20
   as main crossing point from slaveholding Kentucky, 138, 142, 146

Pearce, William, 87
Peg Leg Joe, 55
Pennsylvania, 14, 22, 42, 170
Pennsylvania Abolition Society, 14
Philadelphia, 83, 94, 123, 128
   destination of Henry "Box" Brown's box, 63, 66
   first black abolitionist society founded in, 15
   protest against colonization movement in, 16, 17
   site of first recorded Underground Railroad activity, 14
Phillips, Wendell, 115, 117
Pinkerton, Allan, 134
Price, John, 22, 23, 170
Prigg v. Pennsylvania, 170
proslavery propaganda, 86, 190–99
Purvis, Robert, 18

Quakers, 12, 14, 68, 148, 152
   abolitionists among, 135, 157, 160
   reluctance to harbor fugitives and, 136–37
   role of, in Underground Railroad, 134, 147

Racine, Wisconsin, 170
Rael, Patrick, 21
railroads, 101, 103
Raisin Institute, 146, 156
Randolph, Thomas Jefferson, 187–88
Reconstruction period, 53
religion, 51, 112, 117
   in black community, 15
   confidence inspired by faith in God and, 96, 101–102, 136
   conflicting beliefs and, 182–84
   consolation of, 162–64
   gratitude for deliverance and, 166–67
   of slaveholders, 100–101, 112–13
   see also Quakers
Reminiscences of Levi Coffin (Levi Coffin), 13, 119, 135
Revolution of 1776, 118

rewards, 38, 42, 57, 75, 95
  for capture of antislavery activists, 146,
    156, 157
  for capture of runaway slaves, 56, 129,
    130
Ripley, C. Peter, 16
Roper, Moses, 59, 83, 106
Ruggles, David, 18
"Run-away Slave at Pilgrim's Point,
  The" (Browning), 116
runaway slaves
  assistance provided to, 44–45, 49–50,
    88–90, 158
    criminalized by Fugitive Slave Act,
      171
    paid for, 61, 142
    penalties for, 11
    provision of clothing and, 148
    reluctance of some abolitionists to
      offer shelter and, 136–37
  confinement and, 68–72
  deception a necessity for, 27, 35,
    85–87, 89, 148–51
  denial of citizenship rights and, 23
  denial of due process rights and, 170,
    171
  destitution of, 139–40, 142, 143
  loneliness of, 36–37
  mixed race, 54, 107
    advantages of, 59, 84, 92
  murder and, 77
  recapture of, 107, 113, 140, 191–95
    desperation caused by prospect of,
      119–21
    outrage of Northern citizens
      concerning, 114–18
    punishment and, 11, 74, 83, 95, 106
    violence used in, 196
  rescue of, 15, 129–32
  see also imprisonment; rewards;
    Underground Railroad
Running a Thousand Miles for Freedom
  (Craft), 94
Rust, B.S., 192, 194, 196

Salem witch trials, 14
Sambo stereotype, 27, 87
Saratoga, New York, 200, 201
Savannah, Georgia, 91, 93, 104
secession, 180, 188–89
Senate, U.S., 172, 181
servants, indentured, 13
Seward, William, 22, 23
Siebert, Wilbur H., 13
slaveholders, 22, 42, 86–87, 118, 190
  anger about runaway slaves and, 124
  attitude toward free blacks, 100–101

cruelty of, 52, 84, 95
escape and insurrection feared by, 27
relationship with slaves and, 34, 97,
  108–109
  pretense of submission by slaves
    necessitated by, 86–87, 149–51
religion and, 112
slaves hired out for wages by, 32, 123
slave patrols, 57, 75, 138, 140, 148
  bounty hunters and, 38
  comparison of slave hunt with fox hunt
    and, 95
  confrontations with abolitionist
    Northerners and, 42
  as forerunners of Ku Klux Klan, 53
  motivation of rewards for recapture of
    runaways and, 56
  threats against Underground Railroad
    operators by, 136
  ubiquity of, 106
slave rebellions, 18, 22, 27
  harshening of slave codes in reaction
    to, 28
  patrols employed to guard against, 53
slavery, 13, 68
  brutality of, 44, 52, 57, 83–84
  decision to escape and, 60, 75–76, 85,
    96, 123–24
    despite pain of leaving loved ones,
      35–36
    motivated by
      injustice of slavery, 32–33
      separation of families, 74
  early objections to, 14
  end of, 25
  hardship of, 54–56
  hiding from, 68–72
  protection considered necessary for, 126
  question of property under the law, 121
  sectional differences over, 14, 23–24,
    181–85
  sexual exploitation of women in, 59,
    68, 109, 152
  see also slaveholders; slave patrols
slave traders, 108
Smith, Gerritt, 17–18, 22, 24
Smith, H.K., 191–93, 195
Smith, Patricia, 15
Society of Friends (Quakers), 135
songs, 55, 59
South, the, 41, 52, 187
  abolitionists perceived as interfering
    by, 171
  difficulty of escaping from, 84
  dreaded by slaves, 108
  escape to Mexico and Caribbean from,
    106

state laws against education for slaves in, 59
support for 1850 Fugitive Slave Act in, 20
tension with North and, 19, 118, 134, 184, 185
South Carolina, 24, 27, 98
Spaulding's Exchange, 191, 192
Stearns, Charles, 60
Stevens, Thaddeus, 24
Still, William, 13, 18, 122, 134, 141
St. Louis, Missouri, 112, 113
Stowe, Harriet Beecher, 13, 122, 125–27, 160, 200
public opinion on slavery influenced by writing of, 20
Thomas Garrett's letter to, 157–59
Sumner, Charles, 24
Superior Courts, U.S., 172, 173
superstitions, 165
Supreme Court, U.S., 23, 170, 186
"Swing Low, Sweet Chariot" (song), 59

Takaki, Ronald, 86–87
Talcott, John L., 193, 195
Taney, Roger, 23
telegraph, 66, 153, 154, 165
Tennessee, 101
Testimony of the Canadian Fugitives (Drew), 43
Thoreau, Henry David, 114, 134, 164–65, 180
Tituba, 14
Toledo, Ohio, 153, 154
Troy, New York, 22, 129–32
"True Remedy for the Fugitive Slave Bill, The" (Douglass), 175
Tubman, Harriet, 12, 22–24, 41, 106, 122
known as "Moses," 123
life story of, 128
rescue of fugitive slave by, 129–32
as Underground Railroad conductor, 124, 134
Turner, Nat, 18, 27
Twelve Years a Slave: Narrative of Solomon Northup (Northup), 200

Uncle Tom's Cabin (Stowe), 20, 160, 200
considered illegal, as antislavery material, 122, 125–27
Underground Railroad, 40–41, 43, 94, 106
importance of Midwest states in, 146
importance of secrecy for, 30, 31, 38

operation of, 138, 141–43, 145, 147–48, 152–55
community involvement in, 144
conductors and, 40, 107, 115, 135
exaggerated role of whites among, 134
included Thoreau, 164–65
included Tubman, 12, 128
Quakers among, 14, 119, 157
secret codes employed by, 59
heroism of African Americans in, 13
hope symbolized by, 123
informal nature of, 11
risks involved in, 136–37
work of caring for destitute travelers and, 139–40
origins of, 13–14
Underground Railroad (Siebert), 13
Underground Railroad Records (Still), 13, 122, 141
United States
end of slavery in, 25
homeland to blacks and whites, 16
mass civil disobedience in, 11
see also Congress, U.S.; Constitution, U.S.

Vermont, 21
Vesey, Denmark, 27–28
Vicksburg, Mississippi, 153
vigilance committees, 18, 115, 123–24, 148, 152
Virginia, 13, 18, 43, 60, 188
Virginia House of Delegates, 187

Walker, David, 16–17
War of 1812, 16
Watkins, William, 17
Webster, Daniel, 180
West Virginia, 38, 39
Whig Party, 180
Whipple, Charles K., 158
Whittier, John Greenleaf, 114
Williams, Asa, 165
Williams, Henry, 164–65
Wisconsin, 21, 22, 170
Woman's Life-Work: Labors and Experiences of Laura S. Haviland, A (Haviland), 146
women, 27, 69, 138, 140, 142
sexual exploitation of, in slavery, 59, 68, 109, 152
vulnerability to punishment equal to that of male slaves, 56

Zion Baptist Church, 143, 148, 152